The Way to Minack
DEREK TANGYE

SPHERE BOOKS LIMITED
30-32 Gray's Inn Road, London WC1X 8JL

First published in Great Britain by Michael Joseph Ltd 1968
Copyright © Derek Tangye 1968
Published by Sphere Books Ltd 1975
Reprinted 1980, 1981, 1983

To my brothers Colin and Nigel

TRADE
MARK

Set in Monotype Plantin

Printed and bound in Great Britain by
Collins, Glasgow

CONTENTS

The Invitation

ONE

'What do you miss?'

George Brown asks questions like an inquisitor. Casual, conversational, lighthearted questions have an urgency to them which makes them appear important.

'What do you miss?'

We have a stable door at Minack instead of a normal front door. It opens into the sitting-room, and near to the point where the top half swings indoors, we have an armchair with a high back. The occupant of the chair sits there comfortably enough, nine times out of ten will sit there safe enough, but there are occasions when the chair has been pushed back a little too far so that the top half of the stable door juts out an inch or two above it; and on such an occasion the occupant, should he get up suddenly, might possibly crack his head against the corner of the door. I remember thinking, as George Brown pressed his question, that the chair was so placed that this could be just such an occasion.

'You must miss something. Everyone misses something. Some section of your life must be unfulfilled. What is it?'

He and Sophie Brown were having a holiday at Lamorna, and they spent much of their time with Jeannie and me. There is no telephone at Minack, no noise of distant traffic, no sign of material progress in the boulder strewn, wild land which gently, then steeply falls to the sea of Mounts Bay. Here is a place which is poised in time. Here the old rocks have observed through the centuries the vanity of man, the fitful moments of his power, ambitions lost and won, the fleeing days of living. The old chimney of the cottage prodding into the sky awaits another gale, another sunny

9

day, another mist swirling in from the south, no different from the others it has faced for five hundred years. There it stands, a welcome and a farewell, sharing a landscape with the untamed, sharing the continuity of time. The years pass and the same moss is growing on the rocks, the same music of the waves plays at the bottom of the cliffs.

'What do you miss?'

I marvel at those who neatly analyse themselves and the rest of us. The motion of living appears so simple after reading the views of the theory-boys on this or that. Summaries of their solutions possess no edge of doubt. A huge house of cards is made to look indestructible. There is no grey in any problem. Reason is king. And although I distrust such exponents of logic, there goes with my mood a certain admiration. I admire their confidence because facts, in my own experience, so often lie, mocking the conclusions based upon them. I am, therefore, unable to pigeon hole myself. I am a don't know. I wend a long way round to find a solution to any problem, and when in the end I come to a decision it is usually instinct that motivates it. An inner force which I do not understand pushes me into action, so that afterwards I have to try and make the facts fit the deed. This, I know, is untidy behaviour and it sometimes lets me down. I find myself saying things, for instance, which do not do me justice. I blurt out a sentence which self-discipline would have made me smother, and I declare something which the listener interprets as the truth.

'What do you miss?' asked George Brown.

'Conversation,' I replied; and knew, in my wish to appear decisive, I was again trivially failing myself.

Jeannie and I had come to Minack, years before, because we had learnt to question the kind of life we had been leading in London. It was, in many ways, an enviable life. We were part of an environment of gaiety

10

and glamour which many people yearn for; and we had been lucky enough to have achieved a measure of those ambitions at which we had youthfully aimed. They may not have been important ambitions, but the gaining of them quelled in us envy of others and removed personal frustrations. We were, therefore, no longer restless. A stage in our lives had been reached when we could have a pause; and we realised that if we were not to recognise the moment we would find pleasure becoming a routine and the edge of any achievement blunted. So at any rate it seemed to us at the time.

There were also our failures. Failure can be tolerable when it is a stepping stone to success, and when it is leading to the fulfilment of a dream. In such circumstances you can ride over failure because you persuade yourself that next time you will have the success you desire. But when success is no longer a beacon to lure you, failure however small it may be, is a pointless tedium. Thus it was with Jeannie and me. Superficially successful we were racing along with the years and gaining no roots in the process; and without roots, we believed, all outward success was failure.

'Conversation,' murmured George Brown, half to himself, fingering the cover on the arm of the chair, 'conversation . . .' And I realised he had guessed I had spoken without thinking.

I looked at him from my kidney-shaped desk where I was sitting. A face that did not possess the obvious emblem of power; a chin which receded, kind eyes, a mouth which did not remind one of an orator.

'Conversation,' I repeated, 'because in the country it is easy to become insular.'

'Which confirms what I felt when I read *A Gull On The Roof*.'

'What was that?'

'I wasn't convinced.'

'How do you mean?'

He had irked me. Here was a challenge I had not foreseen. He had read my book, I had already realised, with care; for when a day or two previously he had met a man whom I had briefly mentioned in the book, he had flattered him by saying within a second of meeting: 'I know all about you!' He said this in a tone of attack. It was in the same tone he answered my question.

'I do not believe,' he said, 'that you and Jeannie really wanted to give up your kind of life.'

It is the woman who makes the sacrifice. It is easy for a man to exchange comfort for the primitive, to brace himself to accept a new way of living, to switch environment; but for Jeannie it meant giving up a suite of offices at the Savoy, entertaining the famous in her role as public relations officer, and becoming instead a housewife in a cottage without running water or electricity. This was ambition in reverse. This was the kind of action which the conventional expect to see fail. Our acquaintances waited expectantly. How long will she last in Cornwall? And over the years Jeannie has been monotonously asked by kinder minded people: 'Wouldn't you like to go back to the life you used to lead in London?'

George Brown found a distraction in bantering me. He envied us too in a way. He and Sophie are utterly devoted; and yet, after this brief holiday, privacy ended for them. ('If anything goes wrong,' he said as the four of us sat together at Minack, the election looming, 'we would like a farm, wouldn't we, Sophie? Somewhere far away . . . so that we wouldn't have to compromise.')

He has no ambition in the conventional sense of the word, he does not scheme for his personal advantage. He is absolutely honest. His philosophy is to immerse himself in

12

the job he has been chosen to do to the exclusion of everything else . . . in the manner of an evangelist.

One day when he was at Minack a reporter called and asked for an interview. George Brown blazed: he was on holiday, why should he be bothered on holiday? And the reporter retreated disconsolately. A few minutes later George disappeared from the room, and soon I found him outside sitting on a rock with the reporter happily beside him. He was sorry he had upset the man. ('I have a bloody temper, I know that,' he said to me once, 'but when I have a row with someone I immediately forget it.' Then he added, smiling, 'The trouble is . . . they don't.')

Achievement has not made him, as happens to some politicians, condescending. He seems always aware that eminence does not sever you from what you always have been; and so lurking beneath the surface is humility. I believe this is the cause of his outbursts, a reaction to self-doubt. He responds quickly to the moods of other people. ('A dull chairman at a meeting often puts me off.') He is loyal, and very kind. He is quick to forgive. He hates feuds. ('The years after Gaitskell died were the most miserable of my life.')

But I felt as I was watching him that I was on the edge of a volcano, and it was not my business to stir him on a matter of such minor importance.

'Like you,' I said quietly, 'we didn't want to compromise.'

He had at this time given up smoking, and he did not know what to do with his hands. One moment he clasped them together, the next he rested them on his knees, then he began toying with the fabric of the chair. Suddenly he said:

'You gambled!'

He said it vehemently as if I had been caught committing a felony. Then he added:

'You had no idea what sort of life you were coming to, no training for what you were going to do!'

We *had* gambled. We *had* no idea what sort of life we were coming to. We had *had* no training. In a rational world such conduct is, I suppose, very foolish.

'Why?' he went on, 'why did you do it?'

Conversation, if it is to come to life, must be challenging; and George Brown, I realised, considered argument as a necessary way of passing the time. He was provoking me, but without malice. He was, at that moment, genuinely wanting to know the sequence of events which led us into taking such a rash, unreasonable step; and he was trying to flint me into defending myself.

I, too, have found myself at dull parties making a sensational remark or asking a pertinent question just in order to stir the pool of dullness. My attitude seldom succeeds in its object because the conventionality that breeds dullness retreats from challenge. I make a remark to awake the commonplace, and the response to it is often so dampening that I too feel dull. I am, therefore, on guard when someone tries to awaken my own lassitude; and I was aware that this was what George Brown was trying to do. In such a situation I am anxious, over-anxious, to be as bright as my companion would like me to be; but if my mood, if my temperament at the moment is engulfed by mental cotton wool I am inclined to conduct myself like an inexperienced schoolboy. I flounder. I react with a foolishness so that hours, weeks, months, sometimes a year later, I remember the moment with shame. A self-inflicted wound which no one else has observed.

'It's a story, I suppose, about a search for values,' I began reasonably enough.

Then I added tartly, as if I were aiming to counter his harmless bellicosity by a version of my own:

'And why should you be interested?'

As soon as I had spoken I regretted my tone. It was unnecessarily provocative. Almost rude. I waited.

'Well,' he said, smiling at my momentary impatience, 'it's now clear you and I have something in common ... but I would like to know what decided you to give up the kind of life you both led.'

TWO

George Brown had disturbed our peaceful pool; and since he proceeded to peer at us week after week from the television screen, from cartoons and newspaper photographs, we were not allowed to forget it. He had succeeded in putting doubt into our minds. Perhaps, for instance, we were wrong to remain remote from the community age.

But ideas are inclined to float in timeless rotation when you live in the country. Unperturbed for the most part by man-made time-tables, you indulge yourself when considering a problem by never coming to a decision. Another spring, another summer, and you will find yourself contemplating the problem of the winter before; and so it goes on unless an incident produces an ultimatum.

More than a year had passed since George Brown had been at Minack before I was faced with such an ultimatum. I received one day an invitation to an elegant literary party in London.

I had once before been invited to a literary party, and the occasion has haunted me ever since. It was a month before war broke out and I had just spent a year travelling the world, and I was writing a travel book. On the way to the lunch the chairman of the occasion asked me to make a speech, and he said that all he required were anecdotes of my journey which would make the listeners laugh. I sat nervously through the soup, roast lamb, pêche melba and coffee, until the chairman rose to his feet.

'John Gielgud,' he said to the expectant few hundred, 'was to speak today but is unable to do so. J. B. Priestley was to take his place but he suddenly had to go abroad. I was then lucky enough to persuade John Steinbeck but three days ago he went down with flu . . . and so we have Derek Tangye.'

The faint applause which greeted this introduction still whispers in my memory. So too does the quiet murmur which followed my anecdotal speech.

It was the end of freesia time at Minack and Jeannie and I were in the small greenhouse which we used for bunching. Freesias in the winter, daffodils in the early spring, tomatoes in the summer . . . that was our routine. It was an inevitable habit that we lapsed into long silences as we bunched, thoughts roaming in our minds as we picked up the blooms automatically, fiddled the bunch into shape, tied it, and placed it amongst the others. A long silence, then one of us suddenly out of the blue would announce a result of our roaming thoughts.

'Truth is always changing,' I suddenly announced on this occasion.

'And what prompts such a sage remark?'

'One moment I'm determined to go to London, the next I'm equally determined to stay here.'

Geoffrey at that moment came into the greenhouse with a basket of freesias, a scented tapestry of colour, and he dumped the basket on the bench and began to remove each small bundle of blooms and to put them into the waiting jar of water. He had been with us early in our time at Minack and I had proposed the toast of the bride and bridegroom when he married Emily who also now helps us with the flowers. But at that time we put our faith in potatoes proving to be the *el dorado*, and we were wrong. Geoffrey had to go after a potato season of great disaster, and it was four years before he was back again. It is easier now. We no longer grow potatoes. We have heated greenhouses and several tons of daffodil bulbs. It is more fun now than when he first came to Minack.

17

'What's so silly,' I said, after Geoffrey had departed to continue his picking, 'is that I'm making a mountain out of a molehill. I realise that. It's almost as if I'm afraid of a few days in London.' I was half talking to myself and Jeannie was silent. 'It's not just getting into a train, having a good time, and coming back,' I went on, 'there are other factors involved.'

'Don't be too serious about it,' said Jeannie.

If you live with someone and there are no office hours to separate you, no other life to lead, one has to be on guard against the groove. There you are, fulfilling the halcyon dream, two people who have come together, the end achieved which you hoped for at the beginning, daylight hours shared, boss to each other; and yet unless you remain separate, each a subtle stranger to the other, dullness sets in. There must be no quenching of conflict. Each sometimes must be misunderstood. Propinquity must not be allowed victory because conventional happiness has been won.

'How insensitive of you to say that,' I said.

'I don't understand.'

'You're mocking me.'

'Of course I'm not.'

The doubts in my mind had made me stupidly irritable. A sudden flare and it was over. But I felt angry with myself for feeling angry.

'I'm sorry,' I said.

I felt, however, as soon as I had calmed down, that my burst of irritation had done me good. It was as if a window had been opened on a stuffy room. I began to see more clearly what was irking me.

'Darling,' I now said soothingly, 'what's worrying me is whether another phase of our life is over.'

'In what way?' Jeannie had ceased bunching for the moment and was holding the flowers untidily in her hand. She wore slim grey pants and a white polo necked jersey with

18

her dark hair touching her shoulders. As always she provided an incongruous touch of sophistication to the artisan world around her.

'Take this invitation,' I said, 'five years ago there wouldn't be any doubt about turning it down. I would have refused point blank to travel to London however glamorous the invitation might have been. Yet here I am today half wanting to accept it.'

'Five years ago you hadn't written any of the books which make hundreds of people find their way here.'

'This so-called success, then, is making me restless, making me wish to see my old self again.' Then I added as if it were a joke. 'I don't think that means any good.'

'You can't go on forever seeing life through a chink.'

'See, you also have changed.'

When we finished the bunching we gathered the discarded blooms, the crooked ones and the short ones, those with damaged petals and warped petals, and brought them into the cottage for our own pleasure; and the others stood in their jars waiting for the morrow when Jeannie would pack them in their long cardboard boxes, and no doubt would call me because she could never take the beauty for granted: 'Come and see this box. It's special!' Then the boxes would be strung together in couples, an invoice made out and attached, and then they would begin their journey to some London home by being rushed to Penzance station for the Covent Garden train. And after that we were commercially minded, and the flowers became like tins in a grocery store. They were earning a living for us, and so the hopeful wait would begin for the letter which, in a couple of days, would bring news of the price they had fetched.

It was nearly lunchtime and I poured out a glass of wine for each of us, and I sat sipping mine on the sofa while Jeannie was asking what I wanted for lunch. 'We've got two cheeses to choose from but not much bread. I haven't had time to make any.'

I made my choice, then heard her say: 'You didn't object that other time we were going to London.'

This was true. But I didn't feel apprehensive as I did now. And in any case we never went.

We had been all ready to go, seats booked on the train, a room at the Savoy, when the Lamorna postmaster arrived at the door of the cottage with a telegram. It read: 'Got donkey, Teague.'

A short while before we had been to a pub near Redruth called The Plume of Feathers whose landlord, Mr Teague, was also a horse dealer. Jeannie while she was there murmured that she had always wanted a donkey; and so Mr Teague, a persuasive salesman, made a note of her casual remark as if it were a firm order. Hence the telegram. Hence also the reason for the cancellation of our visit to London.

For Jeannie was not the kind of person to ignore such a telegram, or to remain unmoved by the plaintive eyes of the donkey gazing at us on our arrival in a field at the back of the pub; and within an hour Penny was ours and on the way to Minack in the well of the Land Rover, nose resting on my shoulder as I sat in the driving seat. It so happened, however, that Penny was in foal, and the foal was expected at any time. We could not leave her, or Jeannie insisted it would be cruel to do so; and thus we stayed, and in due course Fred was born. The donkey who cancelled a holiday.

Jeannie's preoccupation with birds and animals was the result of her natural kindness. She wanted to like people but she had found that people sometimes let you down, animals never; and so she felt secure when she gave them her trust. I, however, have never become emotionally involved with them in the same way as Jeannie. An unhappy animal story in a newspaper, and she is part of it; and I have learnt now to tear out such stories before she has a chance to read them. Nor have I ever set out to acquire an animal in a deliberate way, like shopping for a piece of furniture. I am aware of my weakness. I selfishly want to avoid the responsibility that an animal inevitably entails; and so they have to come to me by chance.

For when, in fact, an animal does enter my life, I am sure to become its slave. I hold out for a while, struggling feebly to keep my independence, then I surrender. So it was with Monty whom I first saw playing bewitching kitten games in Jeannie's office at the Savoy; and so it was with Lama, the once wild little black cat who became his successor. So also with Boris, the Muscovy drake, who was unwisely offered as a dinner to Jane, the girl who was then working for us, by a young farmer who was courting her. So also with Penny and Fred; and, more remotely, with the two gulls Knocker and Squeaker who have for years held firm to their rights of the cottage roof. All of them arrived without an invitation from me. It was always Jeannie who first made them welcome.

This capacity for kindness was the secret of her success at the Savoy. She drew to the hotel and to the others in the group, Claridges and the Berkeley, an international set of socialites, show people, politicians and newspapermen who were constantly surprised, sometimes disconcerted, that they were meeting someone who had none of the harsher characteristics of a career girl.

'You wouldn't think she would say "boo" to a goose,' wrote one columnist.

'The prettiest publicity girl in the world,' wrote another.

Her offices on the first floor, past the foyer lift on the right, up the green carpeted stairs, along the corridor and nearly opposite the outwardly ancient looking lift that once was called 'the moving room', were the meeting place of the currently famous; and the walls were covered by photographs signed affectionately by household names. Once a secretary in

21

that office she became, before she was twenty-one, its centre. And when an official history of the Savoy was written a year or two ago, Jeannie's *Meet Me At The Savoy* was in a special section of the bibliography along with two others; one was by Compton Mackenzie, the other was Arnold Bennett's *Imperial Palace* which was based on Savoy personalities of Arnold Bennett's time. She wrote her book when first we came to Minack; and as she was a wayward writer who looked hopefully for distractions, I used to lock her in the chicken house which we had converted into a spare bedroom. 'There's another hour before she can come out,' I would explain to a bewildered caller; and Jeannie would continue her typing. The same rough treatment has recently been repeated; and the result is her novel *Hotel Regina*.

She had shown no wish to return to her glamorous way of life since she had been at Minack; nor, for that matter, had she used the threat of wishing to do so as she might have done during some period of stress. Yet content as she was in the soothing, peasant way of living we had chosen, it was to be expected that a time would come when sophistication lured her again; and so perhaps it was reasonable for me to suspect that she was pushing me to accept this literary invitation. A relief from cooking, a change from bunching flowers, a reacquaintance with her other ego; clothes, wit, flattery, trivial gaiety, style, pace, another world. I could not blame her.

There was also the atmosphere of the Savoy that she should wish to sense again; for behind the lavish facade there is a strange heart. It imposes on those who work there the old-fashioned qualities of pride and loyalty, and these weave such a compelling tradition that even the humblest kitchen hand who can boast, 'I was at the Savoy,' possesses a passport to a job in any hotel in the world.

There is also another form of this freemasonry, and I have been a victim of it many times. Jeannie and I will visit a strange restaurant and suddenly Jeannie discovers that the maître d'hotel or a chef or a waiter spent part of his career at the Savoy. I know then that my meal will be indefinitely postponed as old, wrinkled faces light up, accents excitedly become even more broken, and legendary names of the hotel world are bandied to and fro. I sit there patiently fiddling with a fork, waiting for the emotional memories to finish, growing hungrier and hungrier; and yet I understand. Jeannie was not alone in her feelings when she wrote:

'The Savoy was my whole life. I became friends with its most important visitors and humblest staff, and I grew to love it with a love that was as strong as it was unreasonable; a love that disturbed my dreams as well as my days until I thought and spoke of nothing else.'

That was the background of Jeannie's life before she gave it up and came to Minack with its paraffin lamps; and she had never been back to stay, and nor had I.

'Admit it,' I said cheerfully after dinner, 'you're pushing me to accept this invitation.'

Jeannie was sitting on the sofa close to the new stove. For years she had cooked on a day and night burning stove but recently we had changed to an electric cooker. The Esse had been dismantled and now within the enlarged alcove, we had a stove we could use as an open fire during the day. Lama, a black, silky cushion, was on her lap, murmuring with purrs as Jeannie stroked her forehead.

'I'm not pushing. Just in favour.'

I had found a pipe, had filled it, and was about to light it. I am one of those who are poor at lighting pipes, and I use one match after another; and having lit it, it soon goes out and I start again. There have been times when Jeannie has gone to an ash tray, counted the matches therein, then jokingly said: 'Fifteen matches . . . all in five minutes!'

On this occasion the flame was abreast of the bowl when

she added: 'You're quite right . . . I *do* want to go to London. We've been away all these years and now we can go back having justified ourselves. We were thought of as crazy to leave. People waited for us to creep back, hoped for it, some of them. But we have stayed and fought, and sacrificed all sorts of pleasures, and been patronised when we've had no money, and have always kept faith in what we were doing .

She paused, and I was no longer trying to light my pipe.

'Go on,' I said.

'I would like to have some gay reward for all our struggles. I remember seeing you in a telephone box on a hot August day in Penzance when a cheque had been returned, and you were begging someone to help you honour it. I watched you clenching your fists, and knew the agony as the help was refused. I will never forget.'

'It wasn't as bad as all that.'

The pipe was out, but I did not mind.

'I want to feel superficial again, absolutely useless. I want to lie in bed and have a telephone beside me and be able to ask for what I want when I like. I want to be idle. I would like to have the fun of being greeted by Vercelli in the Grill, or walking into Claridge's and being welcomed by Luigi as if I had never been away, or going to the Berkeley and seeing Pelosi. All the gay things I used to do.'

'I understand.'

She was on cue for a fling. I could see that now. For years every penny that had been available had been spent on the flower farm; a new tractor, endless repairs to existing machinery, three or four years and another new tractor, vast capital outlay on daffodil bulbs, another greenhouse, heaters, oil for the heaters, and all the other mundane things we had to acquire to keep our business moving. Necessary, of course, but it had been Jeannie who had to make most of the sacrifices so that we could afford them.

24

'Well?' she said, smiling up at me.

Lama jumped to the floor and meandered over to the bookcase. There she sat, face looking upwards, hinting that she would like her saucer filled. Jeannie was quick to respond.

'I'm more solemn than you,' I answered, laughing, 'I wouldn't go to London just to be pampered.'

'You get that here,' she said mockingly, 'who cooks for you and does your laundry and supervises all your comforts?'

'The oldest stick to be used by women against man,' I said, realising she had scored a bull's eye, 'I submit, I beg your pardon. You deserve all the flippant hours you can get.'

'Thank you. I'll remember.'

She had filled Lama's saucer and had moved into the tiny kitchen. The kitchen had been her own design, and she had had it made soon after her mother had died . . . her house-proud mother who always marvelled how Jeannie managed so gaily to have people to stay under the then primitive conditions.

But that was in the old days. The new kitchen was like a galley in a boat, indeed it was made by a boat builder from Newlyn, and cunningly designed within a section of the sitting room . . . only ten feet long with a three-foot-wide standing space, a refrigerator, a sink, the electric cooker, and small cupboards of natural wood up to the ceiling. She used to potter about there too much sometimes for my liking. I would begin a mono-logue, then be mildly vexed by her lack of attention. 'I'm listening,' she would call amidst the clatter of pots and pans and water filling the sink. I would doubt it, and cease my talk, and wait until she had finished. No reason to be impatient on this occasion. She was out of the kitchen within the minute.

'You see,' I said, 'I want to find out whether this phase of our life *could* be over. You said yourself one can't forever go on seeing life through a chink.'

25

'Don't take me too literally.'

'I'm not, but I have to admit you made a good point. I'm wondering whether we have become too parochial, too self-satisfied with the rhythm of our life.'

'Why feel guilty just because you're happy?'

'Do you remember Christopher Buckley all those years ago,' I said, ignoring her question, 'when he was chief foreign correspondent of the *Telegraph* standing at the window of your office just before he went out to Korea and was killed?'

'One grey, wet afternoon.'

'He stood there quoting the lines from Barrie: "Do not stand aloof, despising, disbelieving, but come in and help . . . insist on coming in and helping".'

It was during the period when Jeannie and I were making up our minds whether to come to Cornwall. A grey, wet afternoon and I was listening to the voice of a crusader.

'We were involved in those days,' I went on, 'we were not standing aloof as we are now. We had struggled our way into the centre of things, and were successful, and were full of promise as long as we kept our nerve.'

'We didn't, did we?'

'Why?'

'We weren't ruthless,' she said, 'and we were too lazy to be cunning, and were hopeless at intrigue.'

'Lacking the ingredients of success.'

'If you like.'

'I suppose we expected too much of other people, expected them to have the standards we believed we had ourselves.'

I saw Jeannie smiling.

'You're having doubts,' she said, 'because you've forgotten what our life was like.'

'So have you in a way.'

'Possibly.'

'Well then,' I said, 'it's time to remind ourselves.'

I suddenly saw the motive for going to London. My restless mood had to be put to the test; and I would be able to do this

Most of the important decisions of my life had been taken in London, and each decision had ended a phase which I thought at the time was permanent. Of course the stress behind a decision is easily forgotten when you are far away from its environment; yet each decision has built another part of you, sharing the responsibility of whatever happens.

I knew, therefore, what I had to do. I would set out to remember the kind of life I used to lead. I would go to see the places in London where I lived, and seek to catch my mood at the time when the decisions were being made. First, 38 Cranley Gardens off the Old Brompton Road where I arrived as an innocent from Harrow to become an office boy in Unilever House; then Joubert Studios off the Kings Road where I spent an idle summer, then 20 Elm Park Lane, also in Chelsea; then I would remember 56 Portsmouth Street, Manchester; then Cholmondeley House where I was to carry Jeannie across the threshold after our marriage; then Thames Bank Cottage at Mortlake where ghosts, I feel sure, will always shout on Boat Race day. All these in their different fashion led the way to Minack.

They could help me now. I would see them reflected against the present. I might then realise that the values I once believed important had no place in the community age. Perhaps this was the cause of my restlessness. Perhaps Jeannie and I were living in a fool's paradise.

We would try to find out.

THREE

A westerly gale was blowing the night we left Minack; and the roar was as if the cottage were a boat, the roof and walls the rigging. Outside, as I carried the suitcases down the path to the car which was taking us to Penzance station, I was pushed so violently by the wind that I had to drop the suitcases and steady myself. Far away across the bay, the Lizard light winked. The darkness hid the outline of the land around me but there in the distance curving towards the Lizard were the lights of Prah sands, Porthleven and Mullion. No sign of what was in between, only the sound of the sea's rage.

It was Sunday evening in the third week of January, and during the day we had wandered around the cliff meadows collecting the odd daffodils which were in bloom, a few from a meadow close to the sea, a few from another which edged the zone, enough to take to London to give away. Geoffrey and his young wife Emily would be in charge, and they would have no difficulty in coping with any daffodils which might become ready for market; and we hoped, too, they would satisfy Lama; and Penny and Fred the donkeys, and Boris the muscovy drake. There were the two gulls also, Knocker and Squeaker, who year after year had strutted along the apex of the roof or sat on the chimney warming their feathers. They, too, would expect the same attention paid to them by ourselves to continue in our absence. 'I'll bake a special lot of bread for them,' Jeannie had said. Over the years they had turned up their beaks to shop bread.

It is supposed that this country is a nation of animal lovers but sometimes I wonder whether this reputation is deserved.

Any branch of the RSPCA will tell you of the dogs and cats that are brought to them to be destroyed because their owners are going away on holiday. Apparently, in the minds of these owners, a domestic animal is an expendable object, useful between holidays. I should add, perhaps, that these animals brought by their misguided owners to the RSPCA may be considered lucky. There are many others which are left to roam the streets; and I have a friend who looks after such as these, who looks after them until he can find another home, keeping them in kennels often at considerable personal expense. He, too, sometimes doubts this country's animal loving reputation. For at Christmas time he will be pestered with enquiries for kittens and puppies ... and by holiday time they will be coming back to him as unwanted cats and dogs. Their time as toys are over.

We ourselves, of course, have always been extreme in the other direction. Foolishly so. There have been many times when we might have gone away for a night or two, only to be stopped by the thought: 'What will happen to the animals?' It was a vague, sometimes irritating, devotion to them; and yet if you live in isolation, no houses, no neighbours to be seen or heard, no constant reminders of the convulsions of conventional civilisation, it is easy for animals to dominate you. You revolve in a small world that is comfortable and reassuring. You are wanted, and you respond; and you receive rewards at many unexpected moments. It is a pleasant kind of domination.

In the days before our departure we fussed according to the varying vividness of our imaginations. We had been so long anchored to our routine of living that we behaved as if we were about to set off round the world. Would it be wise, we considered earnestly, to let Boris continue his roaming in the neighbourhood of the cottage, or should he be kept locked up in the hut which was his normal sleeping quarters? Boris's range of activities was limited. When first he came, seven years before, we were warned to expect him to fly the district enquiring for a mate; and we were advised to anticipate such adventures by providing him with a mate of our own choice. We did not do so because, in the first place we soon found that Boris had no ambitions to fly; and in the second, we cared not for the idea of endless little ducklings growing up to be eaten. Hence Boris remained a happy bachelor and free to roam as he liked.

He had a congenial routine. He would waddle to his hut in the wood on his own in the evening, and before nightfall one of us would lock him up. He would be let out in the morning and woe betide us if we were late, for then he would hiss and wave his head like a cobra; and if I were the one at fault I felt forced to apologise. 'Sorry, Boris,' I would say, 'I overslept.' His roaming, at first glance, seemed harmless enough because he never went further than the small section of land which surrounded the greenhouse in front of the cottage . . . apart from his ponderous walk up the path to the cottage door where he waited for any titbits which Jeannie was prepared to give him.

The trouble was that the foxes could watch him. For years, in a curious misguided way, we had never feared the prospect of a raid on him. The foxes, we knew, wandered about the field on the other side of the shallow valley and indeed they had given us much pleasure from time to time . . . especially the summer they chose to raise their cubs from the earth they had dug in a corner of the field. But we never thought they would have an eye for Boris until a well-meaning gentleman came along and put the idea into our heads. 'Do you mean,' he asked incredulously, 'that you allow the drake to wander unguarded? It's amazing that a fox hasn't got it long ago.' It was at that moment that innocence turned into anxiety. Darkness, we appreciated,

30

was an obvious danger and hence our care to lock up Boris at night. But in daylight we had always felt that Minack was magically safe. We believed, or more accurately Jeannie believed, that there was a truce between Minack and foxes and badgers in the neighbourhood; and provided we did not allow anyone to persecute them, the vulnerable members of the Minack community would be spared.

A fox, indeed, had shared a winter in the stables with the donkeys; and Jeannie pretended that it was the cub she had once looked after whose paw had been caught in a trap. Every night it got into the hay alongside the donkeys, then slid away around breakfast time. Sammy, we had called the cub; but the fox was a vixen and she became Samantha. Many a time that year I heard Jeannie going down the path which leads to the sea calling: 'Samantha!' ... with a plateful of food. And as many times I saw Samantha appear from behind a hedge, waiting, watching ... but not running away. She could trust Jeannie. No wonder we had believed Boris was safe.

The same threat applied to Lama. She, too, never wandered any distance and was always ready to come in soon after nightfall, but just about the time we were warned about Boris, we were told what had happened to a cat at Sennen Cove adjoining Lands End. In broad daylight a fox was seen to sneak into the car park outside the pub, and snatch the pub's cat which was sunning itself on a wall. Out dashed the pub's customers like a pack of hounds, chased the fox up the road where it soon dropped the cat, badly mauled and minus a tail. We had known of foxes catching cats before, but never had we known so graphic an incident. It alarmed us.

For Lama herself believed she was immune from danger. When she first came into our lives she was a wild cat ... so wild that I remember her hysterically flinging herself against the mesh wire in the chicken run where I had surprised her, in order to escape from me. She had been born in a cave down among our cliff meadows close to the sea, and when she was old enough she began to roam in the neighbourhood of the cottage. She kept always at a distance and Jeannie despaired that we should ever become friends with her. Then one day, a stormy day, we heard a cry at the door. It was Lama. From then on, a change in her serenely took place, and she became an indulgent, home happy little black cat. A strange transformation. A cat which once sped away when anyone came within a few hundred yards of her, became placid and amiable and very loving.

It was this loving which caused us concern. It was as if she believed a magic protected her from danger. A car or a tractor, for instance, was no threat to her and she would contentedly sit in its path. I saw her once advance towards a fox cub which was peering at her from a short distance away, a sauntering, friendly advance. And more recently, indeed only a week or so before we heard the story of Sennen Cove, I witnessed an incident which startled me.

I had gone into the wood near the cottage where Boris had his hut when I saw a young fox weaving about in the grass a few yards away. It was neither a cub nor a fully grown fox. It was elongated like a teenager, and it gave the impression that it was unsure of itself. Head down in the grass for a moment, front legs spread out like a puppy wanting a game, then upright again with head on one side in puzzlement. I stood there absolutely still, and for the life of me I could not guess what was happening. Perhaps it is playing with another fox, I said to myself. But suddenly the fox turned round and darted off into the undergrowth, and for a second I saw a black dash on its tail. Lama, of course.

Lama, therefore, courted danger without knowing it, and this we had to accept. So also did Boris; and thus we had to weigh up the hazards against the inconvenience caused to them both if they were kept shut in. They would be furious, that was certain; and after all, we said to each other, we might impose the same standard of caution on ourselves. A legion of buses were waiting to run us over.

Hence, we decided, our caution in regard to them could become a neurosis, and it would be kinder to allow them during daylight hours to continue their wandering ways. In any case Geoffrey would never be far away. He would be, we felt sure, an admirable guardian.

Penny and Fred, the donkeys, posed a different problem. Nobody was likely to attack *them*. In their case boredom was the enemy. They liked to have us around during the course of the day, liked us to be there if they felt in the mood to be taken from one meadow to another; and if we were not present to obey their whims, they were provoked into taking action. Such action, of course, depended upon the opportunities that might be available. A hiker, for instance, who might pass their way, knapsack hoisted on his back, was likely to feel as he marched head down intent on his journey, a curious sensation around his shoulders. It would be Fred. Fred had developed a technique of creeping up behind an unsuspecting walker, then pushing his nose into the mysterious contents of the knapsack. If there were no knapsack, if the passer-by took no notice of him, Fred would play the 'you're a ghost' game; and this meant that the unfortunate stranger suddenly found a donkey barging at him as if his presence did not exist. Fred found this very funny.

Penny's boredom was exorcised in other ways. Apart from her tuneless, excruciating hee-haw – a sound which was intended to make us rush to her help from wherever we might be in an anguished desire to stop it – she had other tricks. Tricks which she had also taught Fred. She was skilled at gate opening, nudging a latch off a hook. And no one was more talented in removing a bar from across a gap. She was an artist in finding a weakness in any field's defences. She was, in fact, a donkey Houdini; and when the trick had been successfully performed she would lead her son on a spree among our neighbour's fields. Such behaviour, as I have said, only took place when they were bored; and it would have to be Geoffrey's job to see this did not happen. Perhaps it would be his most difficult job, though fortunately he could have some help. 'I'll bring Julie and Philip here,' he said, 'and that will keep them quiet.' Julie was six, Philip four.

'Penny is mine,' Julie had always said.

'Fred is *mine*,' Philip had always countered.

When, therefore, we entered the night train at Penzance we believed we had done everything possible to cater for the idiosyncrasies of those we had left behind. There was food for them galore. We had anticipated their whims as best we could. The security measures were reasonable; and Geoffrey had been primed to forego any normal useful work should any of the creatures display a need for special attention. None of them had any reason to notice that we had gone away. We would have a complete rest from responsibility. Two slaves on holiday. And I had to admit to a great sense of relief. I do not think the train had rumbled along the lines as far as St Erth, before I said to Jeannie in a neighbouring sleeper:

'I feel my London ego is already taking over.'

I heard her laugh.

'Mine is doing the same,' came the reply, 'and by tomorrow I'll feel the Savoy is my natural home again.'

FOUR

I lay awake and listened to the rattle of the train and the occasional toneless hoot of the diesel engine. Camborne, Redruth, Truro. My old home was near Newquay and the station we used was Truro. As a child I never went to Penzance, though Penzance was of enormous importance to my childish self. I used to pretend that Paddington, Penzance and the Cornish Riviera Express combined together in some strange way to represent the journey of life. Heaven knows how I came to make up such a fantasy but for a long while it remained for me a delightful, secret game. Penzance was the mysterious beacon, a never-never land. And there I would be on Truro station either waiting for the Cornish Riviera to come up the line from Shangri-la, or watching it leave the station to go there. I think I had the idea in my mind that life would be as simple as that journey; scheduled stops punctually reached, courteous behaviour, unchallengeable values, a certain aura of romance, and a far-away moment of orderly conclusion.

On the platform of Truro station are the ghosts of my father and mother; and many greetings, many farewells. We would drive from my home, Glendorgal, in an old Wolseley tourer with me in the back, my old sheep dog beside me, my father and mother in front; my father in a large tweed motoring coat and a cap, my mother beside him with her Maltese terrier on her lap, and the three of us trying to talk naturally in these last few minutes before I went back to school. Or they would be waiting for me when I returned for the holidays, and when I leant out of the train window I would see them standing together with sheep dog on lead ready to bark wildly as soon as he saw me, and Maltese terrier tucked in my mother's arms. Safe days.

I was lucky in my parents. They were completely unselfish as far as my two brothers and myself were concerned and they repeatedly, by sacrificing their own enjoyment, helped us along our way. I am afraid that of the three of us I was the most unsatisfactory because I provided no evidence to counter the verdict of my Harrow housemaster who declared to me one day after I had missed a catch in an inter-house cricket match: 'You're useless to society, old man.'

My brother Nigel, for instance, who has now created out of our old home a famous hotel, won the King's Dirk (equivalent to the Sandhurst Sword of Honour) as a naval cadet at Dartmouth. My brother Colin was head of his House and captained Haileybury at Rugby football. Both were older. Both provided an incentive for me to achieve something of equal youthful importance. I knew that this was hoped for by my father and mother.

But I achieved nothing. I failed at the most simple of examinations, and except for a morning glory moment at the age of fifteen when I was captain of the junior football and cricket teams of my House, I provided only enthusiasm to my schoolboy sporting activities.

I had, however, an excitement for living, and this found an outlet in a correspondence course for journalism which I studied after lights out at the bottom of my bed with the aid of a torch. This secret gesture of protest against the teaching methods of my expensive education gave me great satisfaction until the proprietor of the course guessed the truth; and thereupon wrote me a kind letter suggesting that the remainder of my course should be suspended until I had completed my scholastic duties. I agreed reluctantly.

I had now to find some other way to divert me from the tedious boredom of my lessons, but in this I was to be frustrated once again. I wanted to find a master who would be my Svengali, someone who would talk to me about literature and history and ways of the past and the civilised beat of living, someone, in fact, who would counter the crude methods which forced me to write out pages of Shakespeare or many verses of the Bible when I was late or committed some other light misdemeanour, thus spoiling my pleasure in them.

Harrow is a romantic school. There are walls and buildings and paths there which remain unchanged from the days of Raleigh and Byron, Sheridan and Peel, Palmerston and Churchill . . . and there are haunting songs which tear the heart in the innocence of their themes. All this I felt, but who was to fill in the details? I plodded at my examinations and when I failed yet again I yearned the more to find someone who would reassure me that failure at eighteen is unimportant. I was asking too much. Then, as now, the pressure on schoolmasters allowed them only to spend time on those with promise, and thus I remained alone with my hopes. Terence Rattigan, the playwright, was in my House at the time; brilliant scholar and cricketer, charming, kind and a conqueror of examinations. I once followed him and a witty classical master up the Hill, though many yards behind, willing them both to pause and see me and involve me in their clever conversation. They didn't.

Thus I left Harrow without an accolade, and at a time when there were three million unemployed. It was then my father received the reward of being kind to a man some years before. My father's friend was in Unilever and by his influential help I was able to exchange my life on the Hill for that of an office boy at the London headquarters. I was immediately filled with commercial enthusiasm and ambition; and I opened envelopes and ran messages with the zeal of a future tycoon.

Jeannie, meanwhile, seven years younger and living twenty miles away at St Albans, was faring more happily. She was clever, and this puzzled her parents. Her father, an extrovert. did not understand a daughter who enjoyed Charlotte Bronte and Trollope and Jane Austen before she had even reached her teens. He had never read any of them. He was a gay man, overflowing with the desire that everyone should be happy; and, he believed simply. that if everyone was generous to each other this could be achieved. But this eldest daughter of his ... he was slightly embarrassed, though proud, by the ideas she had. 'She's a bit of a blue stocking.' he would explain apologetically. Jeannie, however. was also an athlete. When she was older she played lacrosse for Hertfordshire, and later she was chosen to play for the South Eastern Counties on the wing. News of this particular honour came through the post, and she rushed excitedly to tell her parents. 'Rubbish,' said her father, thinking of his blue stocking daughter, 'it's a mistake. They've chosen Barbara not you. Go and ring the captain and tell her.' There was no mistake.

Barbara was her younger sister and she was very good at tennis. One summer, fellow members of the local tennis club kept urging her to bring sister Jean along ... it was the summer that a young girl called Jean Nichol (spelt with an h) had been chosen to play for the Wightman Cup. At last Jean Nicol (without an h) agreed to go to the club, and was overwhelmed by the enthusiasm with which she was greeted: and she was astonished, when she reached the court, to find that an audience had gathered to watch her. Jeannie may have looked slim and pretty but her play was deplorable. She was a rabbit. She was the Nicol without an h.

This tale of mistaken identity followed Jeannie around; and although she never appeared on a tennis court again, she was constantly being asked about her Wimbledon and other championship experiences. Soon there was to be a climax. Jean Nichol and Jean Nicol became engaged the same week, were married within a few days of each other, and each had the Savoy Hotel as their headquarters. The Press wanted to photograph them together but Jean Nichol refused to meet my Jean ... though it did not stop a confusion over wedding presents.

Jeannie came into my life a long time before I met her or had heard of her. A series of strange coincidences.

When, for instance, I was at Harrow I used to stay with my aunt in a pretty Regency house called Rutlands, set in a large garden, at Bushey Heath. Jeannie's father happened to pass by this house about this time, and from the moment he saw it he had a passion to buy it. He never did, but often he would say: 'Let's go for a drive and see *my* house.' And off the family would go in the car to Bushey Heath; and stop close to Rutlands. I was probably there at the time.

There were other coincidences. My parents, when I was a child, used to let our home, Glendorgal, during high summer, and we would go abroad or rent a house during the same period. I never quite understood the financial advantages involved, I was too young to do so in any case, but I knew that my parents felt triumphant if they let Glendorgal for X guineas while living somewhere else for Y guineas.

One summer a Y guineas house was in Newquay itself, a squat Victorian house in a row almost opposite the entrance to the Newquay Golf Club; and overlooking the patch of green where for decades all-in wrestling had taken place. How could it be that Jeannie's parents should take the same house? They did one summer, and it was in Newquay harbour that Jeannie first learnt to swim.

A schoolgirl memory of Jeannie's is when she went to Holland and Germany along with other members of her school at Westgate. The Westgate school was run by a Miss

Weber and her brother had a language school in Bonn. My brother Colin was at this school though, needless to say, Jeannie did not know this when she visited it.

Her first job was as a secretary in the firm that ran the Dorothy Dix column for the *Daily Mirror*. Jeannie remembers saying to herself as she saw my photograph on advertisements decorating London buses: 'What has *he* done to deserve all this?' Her doubts were justified. I had done *nothing* to deserve it.

Barbara was also now working in London, and she and Jeannie used to travel back to St Albans in the same train in the evening. They would arrive at St Pancras at different times, and so there was a standard arrangement to meet on the platform opposite a certain advertising poster. It advertised Tangye hydraulic jacks.

My own contribution to this series of tentative steps which brought us together took place on a Japanese cargo boat bound for Hong Kong from Sydney just before the outbreak of the 1939 war. A passenger aboard, an engineer on his way to a job in Hong Kong's dockyards, fancied himself as an amateur palmist. For some days I scorned his boastful claims and refused to accept his offer to read my hand; but one evening, after I had had my fill of saké, I yielded to his insistence. I myself was on my way to China, Japan, then home by the Trans-Siberian Railway; and I had a vague hope that this man would be able to tell me whether my journey would be completed before the inevitable war broke out. I held out my hand. 'You're going to marry in 1943 and the girl will be smaller and darker than yourself,' he said, 'and her initials will be J. E.'

This information at the time gave me satisfaction. A girl with whom I considered myself in love had waved good-bye to me at Waterloo Station when I set off on my tour of the world; and she was smaller and darker than myself, and her

40

Christian name also began with J. The engineer had given me good news, I said to myself; and good news it remained until a few weeks later I had a letter to tell me that the girl concerned had married.

The prophecy remained submerged at the back of my mind, but I certainly did not pay any importance to it; it was only an item in my diary. Jeannie, meanwhile, had become a secretary in the Press Office of the Savoy, then had been promoted to Public Relations Officer when her boss was called up. It was there that I first met her. The bombs were monotonously falling on London, but I had had a book called *Time Was Mine* just published; and I was in the Savoy foyer one evening when someone pointed Jeannie out to me. 'A girl of influence,' I was told, 'you ought to know her.' Her sphere of influence lay partly in the Savoy bookstall; and when, after our introduction, she arranged that the book should be prominently displayed on the bookstall, I felt that manners allied to desire warranted me inviting her to dinner.

Carroll Gibbons, at this period, was playing in what is called the River Room. The windows, overlooking the Thames, were boarded up as a protection against bomb blast; and men and girls danced there at night in uniforms of many different European nations seemingly unaware, just as Carroll and the famous members of his band pretended to be unaware, that death danced with the music. I sat with Jeannie against the wall beside the entrance, and once when Carroll passed us he asked in his drawl what Jeannie would like him to play:

'The Lady is a Tramp, of course!'

We had before us roast duckling in red wine sauce, peas and potato croquettes. We had also a bottle of claret. Already we had performed the first fencing of conversation Polite noises had been interchanged and we were relaxing.

My book, I was saying to myself, had brought me luck which was quite unexpected; one question about each other, and another; and then came a wild impulse to ask her what other names she had beside Jean.

'The ghastly name of Everald,' she replied innocently.

I looked at her across the duck.

'Do you mean your initials begin J. E.?'

'Yes. Why so anxious?'

Why indeed. How could I possibly tell her that a prophecy had begun to be fulfilled? Here I sat attracted, at the stage of getting to know her, trying to impress her, diffident because she was a girl of experience, and yet firmly written in my diary were the letters J. E. . . . the girl I was going to marry. I gobbled my duck, made an excuse and went out to ring my best friend. 'I've just met the girl I'm going to marry,' I said, giving him the details. 'Forget it,' he replied grumpily, 'it's war time. Be happy this evening.'

I fell asleep when the diesel broke down outside Bodmin Road station. A wonderful silence had come to the compartment, and I heard an owl hooting, and I began to remember the trees in which it lived, the trees which towered over me as a schoolboy when I fished the river for trout with my father; the river which twined beside the railway line . . . I thought of the car being parked by the station, pulling on my clumsy waders, fixing my rod and line, opening the small aluminium box containing my flies, and wondering which to try first, and then marching beside my father to the river hoping that all the trout in the neighbourhood would soon be deceived by my cast. I remembered . . . and fell asleep.

And so deep was my sleep that I did not wake again until the sleeping car attendant woke me up with a tray of tea and biscuits three quarters of an hour before we entered Paddington.

42

I got up and pulled down the window shutters; and soon, after all the years, I began to see London again.

Cranes. I saw these first. Huge, Frankenstein cranes straddling the skyline like monster crabs. Then, as the train dashed through Ealing and Acton, I saw the early morning commuters posed on the platforms, stiffly in lines like matchsticks; and they were black as well as white. And I thought with mild surprise that during the years I used to live in London a coloured man was an oddity. The train was slowing, and now it was no different from when last I came to Paddington. I was passing the same debris of buildings, the same seedy tall houses, the same grime, and broken windows. All the years of talk and nothing had been done. Time was standing still for me. Coming into Paddington that morning was like arriving there in the years after the war. Only the steam engines were missing.

'To the Savoy!' I said to the taxi driver, after we had taken our turn in the sleepy-eyed queue. And to Jeannie I said: 'I feel nervous . . . like a farmer up for Smithfield Show!' And already unknowingly I had made my first mistake. I had been so impressed by propaganda concerning inflated London prices that I read the scrawl for our tea and biscuits as eight shillings. Only later did I learn it was three shillings. A countryman on the loose. My London ego required time to acclimatise itself.

There is something opulent about the leather smell of a taxi, and now we were speeding through Bayswater and on into Park Lane, I felt the excitement of our adventure. An early morning in London, no traffic, no one yet to crowd the pavements, Jeannie at my side, familiar sights to please, the Vickers building and the Hilton to shock. I was nervous but very happy. I was, for instance, about to wear the cloak of a millionaire. Money was about to lose its control of me. Along Constitution Hill and into the Mall, then round

43

Trafalgar Square and into the Strand. In a minute we would be turning into the Savoy courtyard. In a minute banknotes would take the place of pennies. I had my arm through Jeannie's and I pressed her hand.

'Oh,' she said as the taxi drew up, and the porter advanced to the door, 'oh, I have such a *delicious* sense of being on the spree.'

We went through the revolving glass doors into the foyer, the familiar pillars, the sofas and chairs to the left where people sit to watch the world go by, the stairs past the Grill leading up to the American Bar; and on the right the flower kiosk, the bookstall where Jeannie had arranged for *Time Was Mine* to be displayed, the counter of the Enquiry Office, and a little further along, that of Reception with suave young men in morning coats already on duty. Ahead were the stairs leading down to the Restaurant and to the corridor off which were the private banqueting rooms and the lift which took guests to that side of the building; and ahead, too, were the stairs and the passage which score upon score of times Jeannie had walked as she went to and from Room 205 which was her office. There, too, were the news tape machines which men pretend to look at while waiting hopefully for an expected companion, and the lift which Bert, the liftman, had never left while the bombs fell, and the alcove of telephone boxes where Abel had ruled in an orderly confusion of telephone calls.

'Miss Nicol!'

The welcome had started. A hall porter in his dove grey uniform came forward. Then another. And this was to continue during the first days, as staff came on to their different rosters. The clerks of the Enquiry Office, the waiters of Grill and Restaurant, those of the American Bar, other people who work behind the scenes . . . another and another would come up to her.

44

A young man from Reception escorted us down the stairs which led to the Restaurant, then turned left along the corridor which led to the far lift. The usual thought went through my mind, looking at the key in the young man's hand; I hope we're not going to be put somewhere at the back. Both of us knew of the subtle way in which the importance of guests was judged. Characters which the outsider assessed as important might be considered by an international hotel as only worthy of a minor room. A secret antenna was always at work. A millionaire or a film star, an established one or a rising one, were surprised sometimes by the treatment they received.

We were on the fifth floor, and the young man turned to his right, and we went along the corridor, and when we reached the end, the key opened the door of a river suite. The Savoy had welcomed Jeannie's return by bestowing a subtle compliment.

The élite the world over try to use their influence to secure suites overlooking the river at the Savoy. They have, apart from their opulence and the immaculate service, superb views of London; and those on the fifth floor are, by tradition, the most sought after. 'We stood at the window of our suite on the fifth floor of the Savoy Hotel,' wrote Charles Chaplin in his autobiography on the occasion he came back to live in Europe with his wife Oona ... 'we stood silent, drinking in the most stirring view of a city in all this world.'

When we were left alone, we too stood at the window. It was huge, like a shop's window, and it was divided into three sections and one section was ajar, so that as we stood there we heard the waking hum of London. Away to our right were the Houses of Parliament with the face of Big Ben clearly to be seen; and across the curve of the river were Hungerford and Westminster bridges. Opposite, and incongruous because it seemed to emerge from a patchwork of

45

haphazard buildings, was the Festival Hall; and to the right of it were the eyesockets of the Shell monolith. Sleek tugs and their barges were busy on the river as the tide was high, and we were reminded again how long it had been since we had lived in London; for the tugs we knew when we had our cottage at Mortlake were as T Model Fords to the cars of today. Below us Cleopatra's Needle peered above the bare plane trees of the Embankment Gardens, and I thought of its curious connection with my family . . . it was hoisted into place by hydraulic jacks invented by my grandfather and his brothers, and one jack lies in the foundations to this day. On the left was Waterloo Bridge, and black beetles were beginning to scurry across it to their shops and offices, and Jeannie remembered how she was once one of them on her way to Room 205. Further to the left, past the spick and span *Discovery*, I could see Blackfriars and the Unilever building into which I once scurried myself. And if it had been clear, if there had been no clinging early morning haze, we would have seen ahead of us the hills, the surprising hills of Wandsworth, Lambeth and Lewisham; and beyond them those of Surrey.

'A good beginning,' I said.

'Marvellous,' said Jeannie laughing. And she picked up a telephone and ordered breakfast.

The elegant sitting-room had orange covers on the sofa and easy chairs, a glass cupboard with old china plates, a writing table, a television set enclosed in a walnut cabinet, two china table lamps, a standard lamp with orange shade, a thick green carpet, curtains of greenish grey; and the bedroom was ten times the size of our Minack bedroom, and there were cupboards galore, and layers of drawers, and the view again over the river; and there was a lobby adjoining the large bathroom with cupboards for my own clothes. At Minack we were confined, and our clothes were crowded into odd corners; and so, unexpectedly, it was space which also gave us pleasure in that first hour at the Savoy.

There was a knock at the door and Louis, the floor waiter, pushed a trolley into the sitting-room and breakfast awaited us. After he left I failed, as I had done many times in the past, to manage the Savoy coffee pot; and I spilt the coffee on the elegant pink tablecloth as I poured it into the cup.

And then I picked up my cup and walked to the window and I heard Jeannie say behind me:

'The last time I saw someone silhouetted against that window it was Danny Kaye.'

Danny Kaye in his hey-day always stayed at the Savoy. Nothing is forgotten. You come back to a hotel room and the last time greets you.

'He was pretending to cut my hair,' she went on, 'and the photographer thought it funny, and he caught the moment, and the picture was published when *Meet Me At The Savoy* was serialised.'

'Yes, he did look funny.'

There was another knock on the sitting room door, and a page boy and two girls from the florists appeared. They were laden with flowers, and the two girls came in to arrange them.

'Jeannie,' I said, looking at the cards, 'five different people have sent you flowers!' I was glad she was receiving the welcome she deserved.

She went later into the bedroom to unpack, and I remained in the sitting room, staring down on the river and the Embankment. I was thinking how pleasant it was to be back in London, free from any sense of involvement. So many of my memories were born of tension and frenzied activity, but now I was an outsider. I was still dependent on others, but I was also remote from them. I could observe the scene instead of being immersed in it. And yet, I said to myself, such soothing thoughts might prove deceptive. Only in brief moments does one think one can ever change. The pace of London could still catch me again. The pace I longed to enjoy when I first came to London, and lived at 38 Cranley Gardens.

I would go there tomorrow, I decided. I would take the Tube to South Kensington, walk up the Old Brompton Road, and turn left at Cranley Gardens. I would see myself again as when I first stared at No. 38; a nineteen-year-old, sheltering behind the safety of *The Times*, along with my parents, my relations, and the rest of the middle class of that era; anything unpleasant, *Times* valuation, being kept out of sight

I would remember again the first phase . . .

The Places

FIVE

There was an oak door at 38 Cranley Gardens. I used to face it late at night when I had forgotten my key, staring at its threatening solidity, wondering whether I could dare ring the bell and, after a jittery interval, have the courage to face my landlady in her dressing gown.

'If you forget your key *once* more, Mr Tangye . . .'

In daytime I used to hurry through the doorway, down the steps between the two massive stone pillars supporting the Victorian portico, and run at speed towards South Kensington station along the Old Brompton Road, past Cranley Place and Sumner Place, past Onslow Square Gardens, past the massive flower arrangements in the window of Wills and Seager, past people going to work more sedately. I dodged the traffic and into the station. I had to catch the 8.26 Inner Circle for Blackfriars if I were to sign on at Unilever House in the black column . . . instead of the menacing red one, reserved for those who were more than five minutes late.

I wore a bowler hat, a black city suit, and carried a rolled-up umbrella. I used to buy a third class ticket, then travel first class; and I would sit, eyeing not the reading matter, but the possible coming of the Inspector. So for twenty minutes I believed myself important, my vanity assuaged . . . until the train arrived at Blackfriars, and I rushed up the stairs and along to the back door of Unilever House.

'Mornin' Tangye,' some voice would say to me from behind, 'mornin' Tangye.'

I sat in a large hall of metal desks, and I was the junior

51

clerk in a section of five. I opened envelopes and ran errands, and copied invoices into a ledger; and was obsequious to the manager, a tall, gaunt man with a black drooping moustache like that of Bairnsfeather's Ol' Bill. I was nineteen years old and my salary was thirty-seven shillings and sixpence a week.

I was keen at that time, and studied business books, and was smilingly alert when the thin-lipped colleague who was the least favourite of my superiors, ordered me to fetch him a packet of cigarettes. I believed a show of willingness was the passport to success. I believed that if I set out to be liked, appreciation of my gifts and therefore promotion would naturally follow. I smiled at everyone, kept my temper when taunted, fawned for praise. I had yet to begin to learn about the mysterious forces that rule a career. I was simple.

The months went by and my promotion did not materialise. My keenness lost its edge, my smile its readiness, and I was now ready for diversions. The scope for these was limited, but one which gave me considerable pleasure was The Walk. I could not take it as often as I would have liked to. My absence would have been noticed.

The Walk was, in fact, a tour of the Unilever building. I briskly marched up the stairs, along corridors, up more stairs, along more corridors; and I did this with an air of such purpose that anyone observing me would have thought I was performing a mission, and not carrying out an escape from boredom. Up floor after floor, then down again, and back to my desk, and my colleagues with their faces close to their ledgers.

The fourth floor was my favourite. This was the floor of the directors, and it smelt of opulence. All the other floors had an anaemic smell which gave the impression of dull efficiency. The fourth floor smelt of spice ... as if the directors with their world-wide influence had ordered one of their companies to produce for that floor an exotic furnishing appropriate to its importance. I never discovered what it was but I can smell it now.

Anyone who worked on this floor, any typist or secretary, possessed prestige ... the élite worked for the directors of course; and when, on my walk, I passed these girls coming out of their sanctums, shorthand notebooks in their hands, lofty, distant expressions on their faces, I was annoyed to find they made me feel insignificant. Could not these girls guess that the young man they saw walking so briskly had been to a deb dance last night with Lady This and Lady That?

I then found that my heart beat a little faster when, going down from the fifth or up from the third, I approached the fourth floor. I felt as if I were about to play a game of roulette, for I had to coincide my walk along the corridor with the appearance of a pretty girl from one of the sanctums; a pretty girl, tiny with Slav eyes, whom I had first seen walking out to lunch with a clerk from margarine sales. Sometimes there was no sign of her; often, miraculously often, she would appear from the door just as I was passing. I would stare at her, my heart would flutter ... and I would continue briskly on my way.

This hesitation on my side to talk to her, apart from any natural lack of courage, was typical of my attitude at this time. I had been brought up to believe that social conformity was the yardstick which ruled the life of a gentleman; and I was that kind of gentleman. When, for instance, my Harrow housemaster bade me goodbye when I left school, he sent me out into the world with this advice: 'Don't be rude to servants in other people's houses.' He pronounced this as if he were giving me the golden key of wisdom ... and I was impressed. His superficiality was reassuring. It seemed to promise that I had only to be patronising towards those with accents rougher than my own for me to have a happy and secure existence. I, and all those like me, belonged to a race apart; and we did not mix with the others.

Hence my corridor courtship, though lasting for many weeks, only left me with unrequited desire. I never met the girl. I never learnt her name. Yet here I am after all these years remembering her, and for a very good reason. My unrequited desire for her, my missed opportunity, dented the confidence in my middle-class standards which hitherto I had taken for granted.

There was another diversion, long talks with Howard Clewes in the basement cloakroom about the books we were going to write.

'A pekinese belonging to a rich woman will be my hero. He will write in the first person about her flamboyant life.'

'Why not write a book from the viewpoint of a shoe lace?'

'I'm going to make an Earl the chief of London gangsters.'

Howard Clewes was a trainee and I therefore considered him a superior person, far superior to a clerk like myself. He was dapper, a high forehead, a neat moustache, a pale face, and a regular feature of his impeccable clothes was a fancy waistcoat, like the type I used to wear at Lords for the Eton and Harrow match. I listened to his ideas with admiration, and I goggled when the following week he would inform me he had, in the meantime, already turned one of his ideas into a novel. I never knew whether he was as industrious and prolific as he claimed. The first novel I read of his was *The Long Mirror*, and that was over twenty years later.

I myself preferred talking to writing; or just dreaming. I found it simpler to pour my undisciplined thoughts into a diary, a scrawling, gushing document which, like most diaries that are written without the future in mind, contained neither truth or lies ... only the flash of the fleeting mood with its consequent omissions.

'I'm so lazy,' says one scrawl, 'and if I don't pull myself together pretty soon I'll achieve nothing.'

I was now twenty.

I had enrolled again in a course of journalism, similar to the one I studied by torchlight under my bedclothes in my study at Harrow. I did so in the hope that the results would provide me with the prestige I so coveted; for, unlike Howard Clewes who wanted to write because he believed he had a tale to tell, I only wanted to write to see my name in print. I had been a nonentity at school, and this irked. I was still a nonentity, and I was determined to correct the situation. I cherished the belief, guilelessly and without a trace of cynicism, that clever, successful people chose friends on the basis of their publicised achievements; and so if I were to gain an entry into this circle, if I were to be part of this sophisticated Nirvana, I had to achieve some sort of notoriety.

My writing ambitions, therefore, though motivated by my instinct were governed by my head. I needed a halo, the same evergreen halo of one kind or another that the young always seek to boost their importance. In my fluffy world of debutante parties I wanted to say I was a writer, not just a clerk. Any kind of writing. Anywhere in print. Anything to create a mirage of achievement. And so when my little articles continued to be returned to me unpublished, the weak moment was certain to arrive when I would pretend. The shadow of myself as a writer would be born.

The occasion when this first happened was at a bizarre party given by Tallulah Bankhead. I had been taken there by a wealthy South American diplomat who himself had begun the evening in an unusual way. He had entertained myself and the other guest, Adrian Daintrey, the artist, to an elegant

55

dinner at his house in Eaton Square; and instead of offering us a cigar when the dinner was over, he suggested a pipe of opium. The three of us retired to an over-furnished room upstairs, the paraphernalia of opium smoking was produced, and in due course there I was puffing away like any old Chinaman.

After a while I said: 'I don't feel any effects.'

'Nor do I,' said Adrian.

'Ah,' said the diplomat, 'you come here often. Get the habit . . . life will become beautiful.'

It was beautiful enough for him that evening to take us uninvited to the hotel where Tallulah Bankhead was staying: and as I entered the suite and saw the numerous faces who previously I had only seen as photographs in *The Bystander*, I said to myself: 'This is it. At last I am a part of high life.' I was indeed. Never before had I seen any hostess of mine dance in such a provocative way before her guests. Nor in my wildest dreams did I ever expect to help carry a cabaret singer of world renown home to her bed. And in between times I had told my lie.

Tallulah Bankhead was a fabulous, lovely eccentric with a husky American voice, possessing little talent except a huge capacity for living. She was of the kind that each decade produces to provide headlines for the newspapers. Everything that Tallulah did or said was news. In an age when there was no television, her face was as well known as the heroine of a TV serial. Her activities astonished and pleased the humdrum. And now I was in her company. And sometime during that evening or early morning, I was sitting at the piano in a corner of the room playing my party pieces of Night and Day, then Stormy Weather, when she flopped her arms around my shoulders.

'Darling,' she asked throatily, 'darling, what do you *do*?'

Out of the corner of my eye I saw across the room a well

known playwright, a comedian in a Cochran revue, two Peers, the leading lady of London's longest running play, the leading man of another, and an industrialist who, I remember reading, possessed the world's largest yacht. I could not possibly admit I was a clerk.

'I write,' I said confidently, playing a fat chord.

'Darling, *how* exciting . . . what do you write? Plays? Have you a play running in London?'

I did not know then that some people ask questions without expecting an answer. I took her seriously, and was out of my depth.

'Oh, no,' I said airily, 'I write for magazines.' Then added in a panic: 'Small magazines . . . like *Answers* and *Titbits*' . . . I writhed at the thought she might ask for more details and I saw myself being shown up as a fraud before everyone present. I had, however, said enough. She had already lost interest and was 'darling-ing' somebody else.

Throughout that summer I was usually bleary eyed when I stared at my ledger in the morning. I was a bright young thing, a deb's delight, and my old Harrovian tie was a passport of respectability among the mothers. I had discovered, meanwhile, that a necessary feature of this form of entertainment was to develop the art of being a snob. Hence when I received the embossed invitation to a dance, along with an invitation from a well meaning hostess to one of the dinner parties beforehand, I would accept the former but dally with the latter. A deb's delight automatically accepted a dance invitation . . . but a dinner party, one of the formal dinner parties that preceded the dance, he was wary about. He did not want to commit himself to a commoner when a day or two later he could have accepted an invitation from a Duchess.

There was, of course, no virtue in such futile society games. No object either, except for the wealthy social climbers. Nor was there the excuse of escapism, because there was nothing these people had to escape from. Three million unemployed was only a figure to them. There was no threat of war to make them apprehensive. No mood of impermanence to make the young jittery. No cause to yell for. A comfortable smugness pervaded the scene. Ramsay Macdonald had deserted the Labour Party and was heading the Coalition. The King was solidly in the Palace, the Archbishop at Lambeth, and the Empire a vague wonder in the far distance. The smugness seemed likely to last for ever.

The season was nearing its end, and I was in a daze of tiredness. I used pointlessly to stay at a dance until three and four in the morning, have four hours' sleep then dash to the office, and often hurry back to Cranley Gardens in the evening to have an hour's sleep before starting the merry-go-round again. All very well to have experienced this kind of life, I said to myself, but what did it mean? Dull girls, dull conversation, and an impatience with myself.

It was about this time that I met the most beautiful girl I had ever seen. She was a ballet dancer and instead of being content with desire I found myself coping with infatuation. This had happened in light fashion to me before. There was one girl, for instance, a fair, pretty little thing who was the first girl I ever took out to a restaurant on my own; but the romance died the same evening. I took her to the Mayfair where Ambrose had his famous band, and the headwaiter observing my obvious inexperience in such a sophisticated world, dumped us at a table for two next door to the drums. The din was awful. The girl and I bawled at each other until two in the morning, and that was enough. I never saw her again.

Pearl was a ballerina of the Ballet Rambert company, but when I first saw her she had a part in a revue at the Comedy Theatre. It was a cosy, undistinguished revue, but there was a

58

number in it called Mediterranean Madness which brought the house down; and in this number Pearl appeared from out of a dark blue backdrop, wearing precious little, and dancing to a sad little song sung by a young man from the side of the stage. I was overwhelmed with emotion. Dark hair to her shoulders, slim body sinuously dancing, a face like an exquisite Oriental, she seemed to me to be a young slave on display. I had to meet her. At any cost I had to overcome the obstacles in my way, and these of course were many. Pearl was the toast of the town, pursued by eligible young men and society hostesses ... and I was a twenty-year-old clerk knowing not a soul who could either fix an introduction or ask me to a party where she would be. Days passed without a solution, and in the evenings I would sit in the theatre gallery and watch her; then wait outside the stage door and see her disappear with some handsome companion. It was agony.

However, after one such evening when I was walking back to Cranley Gardens, I had a bright idea; and the next day I put it into effect. I reckoned that her admirers competed with each other in the amount of expensive flowers they gave to her, huge bouquets, dozens of roses; and so if someone sent her only a few, the very parsimony of the gesture might make her sit up and wonder. I therefore despatched six red roses to the Comedy Theatre along with a note of admiration and I added, this being the real purpose of my gesture, an unconventional request. Would she meet me at six o'clock the following Thursday at the Berkeley for a pre-theatre supper?

I arrived fifteen minutes early and my heart was thumping so loudly that I felt embarrassed. Surely all these people sitting around on the sofas must hear it? I looked at their faces and envied their nonchalance. Thump, thump, thump ... ten minutes, five minutes. Would she come? Or had she thrown my note away and made a joke of it among her gay friends? I fingered the red carnation in my button hole. I had explained in my note that I would wear one so that she would be able to recognise me. Panic ... supposing some other young man was also wearing a red carnation? I looked wildly round ... then suddenly, there she was. A slender dark figure wearing a black velvet dress, and more beautiful than even I had expected.

I suppose it was inevitable that the meeting would not be a success. We had a table in the alcove at the back of the restaurant, and as soon as she sat down she said: 'I think I am mad to have come here.' This unfortunate beginning only increased my nervousness, and my mumbling conversation did not make sense even to my ears. Nor did she make any effort to help, and I looked at my watch and saw half an hour had gone and there was still another half an hour before she had to leave for the theatre; and I wished I had never sent the roses and that I had kept my illusion. There she sat, polite, cool, exquisite, and I was thankful when Ferraro, the old maitre d'hotel, came up to the table and began talking to me. At least his gesture gave me *some* position. I knew him well, and knew also he sometimes said more than he should. There I was keeping him beside us as if he were a lifebelt when I casually mentioned that I was wondering whether to dash down to my home in Cornwall for the weekend.

'Ah,' he said, looking coyly at Pearl, 'I expect it all depends whether you say yes or no tonight.'

I never expected to see her again. I went to bed miserable, woke up miserable, and consoled myself that I had added something useful to my juvenile experience. I felt lonely. I even looked at my ledger with affection, as an object that was familiar. I went on my walk round the Unilever building and hoped to see my girl of the fourth floor emerge from her sanctum . . the sight of her would have given me comfort And then two days later when I got back from the office, a letter was waiting for me. Pearl had thanked me. Then, of course, my agony started all over again.

It is the sweetness of youth that weeks are months, and months are years; and the real years are far, far away on the horizon. I knew Pearl for a year and a half, and it seemed a lifetime. And when we no longer had anything to offer each other, and friendship had become dull, there was a comical sequel.

My brother Nigel was three years older than I; and this meant, as far as I was concerned, that he wore the mantle of a sage although, in fact, he was only twenty four years old. He had a vast amount of talent, a musician, an artist, brilliant and witty, and after beginning his career as a naval officer, he resigned and went into aviation. He became in due course an instructor at the old Stag Lane aerodrome near London, and one of the finest aerobatic pilots in the country. He was wonderfully good looking, and one day when Alexander Korda had called him in to advise on the flight sequences of *The Shape of Things to Come*, H. G. Wells saw him in the studio.

'There he is!' the squeaky voice cried out, 'there's the man I want to ride naked on a horse at the beginning of the film!'

Possessing such qualities, and glamour, as he did, I was always a little apprehensive as to the impression he might make on the girls I myself fancied. I had a fright one night, for instance, after taking Pearl home to the flat where she then lived in Hanover Square, when I observed a Morris two-seater with canvas hood slowly circling the square. It struck me immediately as familiar, and I hid in the shadow of St George's Church to watch it pass by. The driver was Nigel.

We were such good companions, however, that when I

came out of the shadow into the road and held out my arm like a policeman we both laughed; and he gave me a lift home. Even so I knew that here was another rival; and when several months later I left London for Manchester, it was inevitable that Nigel should take Pearl around. I did not mind. Nor did I mind when that Christmas he brought her as a guest to our home in Cornwall. So often I had wanted her there but she had never been able to arrange it; and now she was in that lovely place as a stranger. 'Ashes,' I scrawled in my diary, 'are sad things.'

But in the meantime I had lost some of my edgy ways, and I no longer felt very young. Pearl led me into a world of people, books and conversation which I had never known before. My values began to change and I was no longer ruled by embossed invitations. Certainties became doubts, and I was the happier for it. At least I was moving. As for Pearl, her sole ambition was to become a great ballerina. She never did, although few who saw her dance will ever forget her. She married a film director, and died in Hollywood when still in her twenties.

One evening I will always remember. I had collected her after the theatre and we were in the balcony of the Cafe Royal. Gay people around us and below us.

'Look,' I said, handing her a copy of a newspaper, 'read that!' It was a copy of the old *News Chronicle*. I waited a minute, then saw her smile.

'The beginning,' she said.

The beginning: five hundred words I had written about archery. My name in print at last.

SIX

I left my two comfortable top floor rooms at 38 Cranley Gardens on my twenty-second birthday, and went to live at Joubert Studios in Jubilee Place off the Kings Road, Chelsea.

My single room faced an alleyway and saw no sun, a lugubrious place; but to me it seemed like a palace because it was another step towards my emancipation. My aim in life at this time was to rid myself of the strait-jacket standards my environment had brought me up to believe indestructible, and to find a way to be free of the restlessness inside me. I had no clue where this restlessness might lead me but, if I bottled it up, I knew I would never find happiness; and so leaving Cranley Gardens meant leaving conformism, and moving to Chelsea meant moving to intangible freedom.

'All I want out of life,' I wrote in my diary that first evening at Joubert Studios, 'is to be able to say at the end of it that I have lived vividly.'

Such a vague ambition suited the situation in which I now found myself. I had been faced with a decision to make. After making a nuisance of myself for months in Unilever, I had been offered a job away from a ledger. Here's your chance, I was told, here's your chance after all your grumbles about still being a clerk in accounts. And the plum I was offered was the position of a salesman of soap in Warrington.

Once I would have been excited by the prospect but the waiting had killed my enthusiasm; and in any case I was wiser. No longer did I see myself as someone dedicated to the pursuit of money, nor did I see any virtue in surrendering one's life to the whims of a great Company. 'A career,' I had read somewhere, 'is like a voyage through a long and winding pitch black tunnel . . . and when you come out of it, of it, your life is over.' A depressing description indeed, but it made me aware, even more sharply than before, that I must follow a career which I could enjoy.

Unfortunately I had no qualifications; and I was now twenty two. I was persistently reminded of these drawbacks each time I obtained an interview with someone of influence.

'I note, Mr Tangye, that you haven't passed any examinations . . . not even the School Certificate.'

'You see, Mr Tangye, without having a University background you are a little old for us to start training you.'

No one inside or outside Unilever had any real use for me. I was given a three week trial in the advertising company of Lever Brothers, writing copy, but this also ended in failure. I applied to other advertising agencies and answered advertisements in *The Times*, advertisements of the type which seek a young man with initiative. I wrote to provincial newspapers, enclosing a copy of my *News Chronicle* article on archery as evidence of talent, and received no replies. I cultivated the friends of friends of men in power, hoping a miraculous meeting might suddenly be arranged with some tycoon who would immediately give me my chance. On one occasion I thought my persistence had at last succeeded. I had manoeuvred an introduction to Geoffrey Dawson, editor of *The Times*, and I found myself sitting in his office in Printing House Square, sunk deep in an armchair.

Geoffrey Dawson, bearing in mind my background, seemed to me to be a god. He had not as yet achieved his footnote in history, that of being one of the arch appeasers of Hitler. His role at the time was simply that of guardian of the Establishment, an omnipotent censor of values good and bad. I was not, of course, concerned with his moral attitudes, I was only concerned with his attitude towards me;

and I sat in the armchair trying to look intelligent while he stood with his back to the fireplace and delivered a monologue.

I have learnt now that famous men periodically like to grant interviews to young people so as to remind themselves how clever they have been. Young people gaping earnestly, believing the interview is for their own good, represent shadows not themselves; and the interview has failed as far as they are concerned even before it has begun. So it was with my visit to Geoffrey Dawson. He had no intention of helping me. I was there only to listen, and to receive avuncular advice. One piece of advice, however, flickered my interest and for a moment I knew I was inside the mind of this editor of *The Times:* for Geoffrey Dawson, bottom to the fireplace, hands in trouser pockets, hard eyes behind a bland smile, suddenly displayed his hate for the Press Lords.

'Remember,' he said, winding up his monologue and speaking with some passion, '. . . remember this advice I give you. You may wish to become a journalist but I warn you, never *never* work for Lord Beaverbrook or Lord Rothermere. Such men would destroy you.'

I was to work for both their newspaper groups.

Meanwhile I had this decision to make. Should I become a soap salesman? It posed me with the perennial problem of youth, the problem as to the extent I should believe in myself; or whether my instinct was mixed up with wishful thinking, a case of bravado, or whether I was wanting to act the rebel just to pretend I had promise. One needs luck at such moments, someone to meet who pushes you; and it happened to me on this occasion in a ridiculous way.

A shop window in Ludgate Circus at this time advertised that it was the home of a phrenologist. There were models of bald heads facing the passers-by with weird hieroglyphics thereon; and placards of promises that the customer who allowed the bumps on his head to be examined would have the trends of his character and talents accurately described

I had been passing this window for the three and a half years I had been at Unilever, on my way to lunch at the Mecca half way up Ludgate Hill; and I had dismissed the extravagant claims as the work of a crank. But now, because I felt vulnerable and puzzled, I was prepared to put them to the test. I had nothing to lose by seeking a bizarre opinion.

And so one lunchtime I found myself sitting in a chair while an old man gently pressed the bumps on my head. It was like a massage, and a quiet haziness was coming over me when suddenly the old man said urgently:

'You must not barter! You must not barter!'

Such a cry of warning at such a moment had, of course, a profound effect on me. He had said exactly what I wanted him to say. And when a few moments later he further declared that my bumps provided evidence that my future lay in advertising, interior decorating or journalism, I was certain an oracle had spoken. No bartering! Journalism! At the cost of a guinea, sitting in an old leather chair with the noise of Ludgate Circus in my ears, I had received the advice I had been searching for. There and then I decided to act before common sense intervened. I returned after lunch to Unilever House, formally refused the job in Warrington; and gave in my notice.

Gestures are wonderfully intoxicating. They provide the confidence which usually somebody else has to pay for. As I stumped out of Unilever House that evening, out of the cavernous doorway into New Bridge Street, I knew I was faced with a predicament. Once my notice had been worked out I wouldn't have a penny. No money in the bank, no income. And so there would be no alternative but to appear to blackmail my father and mother into helping me. That night I sent off a letter of explanation to my home in Cornwall; and began the nervous wait for a reply.

My parents were conventional in so far as they believed that there were certain standards, if maintained, which ensured a contented life. My father, for instance, had a sense of duty towards both his family and the community; and he would deny himself some pleasure time and time again in order to fulfil that duty. He was poor by middle class standards of the day; and one of my most vivid memories is the sight of him in his cramped study at Glendorgal, poring over papers and account books, trying to make one and one make three. He was always travelling to London and Birmingham, and such travelling he loathed. He had, however, a duty to perform in trying to help save our old family engineering firm; and this he succeeded in doing though it was years afterwards, after he died, that it paid its way again He had no income from this source, nor was he paid as chairman of the Cornwall Quarter Sessions; and so one of the reasons he travelled was to earn money as a part time London traffic commissioner, a responsible job which he gained not only because of his reputation but his past, long ago, experience as a barrister.

He was very fond of music, particularly opera. He had joined up at the outbreak of the First World War, giving up his career as a successful barrister; and at the end of that war he decided, wrongly probably, not to return to his Chambers in the Temple but to continue to serve as an Intelligence Officer in BAOR of that time. Thus my young years were spent in Cologne, in a huge house on the embankment opposite the Bismarck statue. It is not the house I remember, however, but my visits to the Opera House. My father took me and my brothers there four and five times a week and, young though I was, I became so emotionally involved in opera music that if I heard an

67

isolated bar being played I was able to recognise from which opera it came. Later, when my brother Colin and I were both working in London, we used to hasten in the early morning to Covent Garden before going on to our offices, put our names on a hired stool in the gallery queue, and see The Ring through together sitting on those hot, hard seats close to the roof. Then sometimes when I was staying at Glendorgal, my father would suddenly rush out of his study where he had an old fashioned wireless set with earphones, exclaiming: 'Come quick! I've got the Milan Opera House!' And, putting on the earphones, I would excitedly hear amid the crackling atmospherics, a faint Scarpia wooing Tosca.

My mother, I feel sure, would have carried a suitcase five miles if she thought it would help one of us. She and my father were devoted to each other, and I never knew them have a quarrel. Yet it was for her sons that she lived, and sometimes she had original ideas how to help us. She once read that someone with the same family name as her own had become a millionaire sheep farmer in Australia. She wrote to the *gentleman* inviting him to visit Glendorgal on his next trip to Britain. In due course he arrived; and his long lost cousin together with her sons were waiting on the Glendorgal doorstep to greet him. We were, of course, on our best behaviour. My mother had primed us that this was essential if her hopes were to materialise. Alas, something went wrong. The millionaire died a knight, but my mother waited in vain for the solicitor's letter she had planned for.

They were both worried when they heard I had left Unilever. Colin was safely in Lloyds, Nigel too was safe because he had proved his brilliance, and so only myself was a problem. The family which had grown up so happily and easily together, with such conventional smoothness, were faced with the odd man out. And yet when I received the reply to my letter telling them what I had done, my father and mother kept their concern to themselves. 'It's your life,' they said, 'and we will do what we can to help.'

I now became ensconced in my room in Joubert Studios with three pounds a week and time on my hands. My room cost me twenty seven shillings and sixpence without breakfast, so I had one pound twelve shillings and sixpence as weekly pocket money. This money was an allowance from my father and mother but it clearly had to be increased, and so I turned my attention to doing so. I had no intention of looking for a regular job because I had the intuition that only by remaining my own master would I gain the end I was aiming for. I had no calculated plan, just a vague belief that the opportunity would suddenly face me; and I had to remain free in order to seize it.

Thus I became a part time salesman first of electric light bulbs, then of ladies' stockings; and I had a splendid trade in both until I had saturated my friends who were householders with electric light bulbs, and my girl friends had lost their sense of humour. The flat racing season had now begun and I noticed one day a particularly tempting advertisement in the *Sporting Life*. A Mr Siebert of Sackville Street offered a foolproof system, the backing of the most newspaper tipped horses; and although this might be considered obvious enough, Mr Siebert had an ace up his sleeve. He had a complicated staking method of his own invention which defeated any sequence of losing horses; and every day by letter post the subscriber would receive the day's method of investment.

I was sufficiently cautious to pay a visit to Mr Siebert's address, and found him, an elderly grey haired man, on the second floor of number Thirty Six wearing a black suit, a high winged collar, and a cravat. He was sitting in an untidy room surrounded by newspapers. He looked bewildered but this greatly impressed me; for here, I said to myself, is an honest man burdened by the responsibilities of handing fortunes to others. He talked softly, reasonably, convincingly, in a broken accent, without boasting; and I left his presence determined to find the necessary capital to follow his system.

My mother and I had been in partnership before. A wayward, charming Etonian friend of mine had induced me, when I was at 38 Cranley Gardens, to put my faith in a greyhound racing system; and we used to visit together the different race tracks night after night. At one period when we were having a remarkable run of success, my mother was also staying at Cranley Gardens; and she became highly enthusiastic when she found me returning from a session at the White City with several pounds in my pocket. She offered to contribute to the venture so that I could increase my stakes and also, therefore, my winnings. I had, of course, no notion that she had decided to carry out a plan of her own.

Almost immediately, on that occasion, we entered upon a losing sequence so long that we were forced to give up the system; and yet the memory of this did not seem to deter her when I mentioned Mr Siebert. I had, however, guessed that she would be impressed that he had his office in Sackville Street; for in those days anyone who had an office off Piccadilly had a special prestige. It inferred that Mr Siebert was an expert; and I knew that experts of any kind, in my mother's opinion, possessed the magic of infallibility.

So my mother and I went into partnership again. Racing day after racing day, an envelope containing Mr Siebert's mathematical calculations arrived at Joubert Studios. Moreover it was not a question of putting the bets on in the morning, then waiting for the results in the afternoon. Mr Siebert's staking system depended on the results of each race; and so my afternoons were spent in hot telephone boxes ringing up my bookmaker and making the necessary adjustments. By the end of April I had begun to lose interest, by the end of May Mr Siebert's envelope had become a menace, by the end of June I could cope no more. We had neither lost nor won a penny, sheer tediousness had exhausted my desire to bet. But my mother's own deep laid plans had succeeded. She had cunningly controlled me while I indulged my fling. I was never to follow a betting system again.

By the end of June I had also become rattled by my mode of living. 'I'm fed up with myself,' I wrote crossly in my diary, 'I talk too much, and I spend hours worrying what people think of me. I'm living aimlessly. I must find a purpose.' I was like someone waiting his turn on the tennis court, performing any frivolous pastime until his name is called. I was, for instance, a deb's delight again but now, instead of being bleary eyed in the office, I stayed in bed at my leisure. This might have been fun had not my conscience continued to prick me. This was a Bertie Wooster kind of life without the money. I lay in bed with my hangover, mentally chastising myself for my misbehaviours of the night before; and I felt miserable and helpless and vapid.

I had, however, a practical consolation for being so annoyed with myself. My weekly funds were quickly spent, and although I was assured of an elegant dinner in the evening I had also to eat during the day. One early morning I was standing at the buffet of a coming-out dance when I observed one of my deb's delight colleagues stuffing sandwiches in the pockets of his tail coat. There was, of course, a pocket in each tail and he was filling both of them, wrapping the sandwiches first in handkerchiefs. He was in the same financial plight as myself, and he explained to me that he always relied on the dance of the night before to fill his larder for the following day.

I mentioned the moral aspect of purloining the sandwiches, but he correctly maintained they would be thrown

71

away once the party was over. His chief concern, therefore, lay in the timing of acquiring the sandwiches, and it was to be mine too; for though we might be morally at ease, we certainly did not want the embarrassment of a hostess catching us redhanded. Thus I learnt it was necessary to wait, before taking action, for the moment when the band had stopped and its members were packing their instruments away . . . so that there was no chance of having to dance with the sandwiches flopping against the backs of my legs.

All went well for several weeks until I became over-confident. One night, instead of waiting for the band to pack up, I surreptitiously wrapped up some sandwiches while the band was still playing, intending to go home immediately they were safe in my tail pockets. I had stuffed one lot away, was pushing the other in my second tail pocket, when my hostess of the evening came gaily up to me and asked how I was enjoying myself. Manners required me to ask her to dance, and I foolishly led her to the floor. At this moment the band struck up Vienna, City of my Dreams, and instead of a shuffling foxtrot, I was forced to career around in a waltz. My partner and I had circled the floor but once when someone called out to me: 'You've dropped something!' And there on the floor, dancers all around them, were my sandwiches.

These untidy frolics had a value because they provided remorse, and out of remorse came introspection. Sometimes I would take a Green Line bus out into the country and walk the day long, asking myself questions I was quite unable to answer. I did not seem to belong to any groove, no banner spurred me. I thought of my friends who were contentedly following a career, and others who lived for the day without a moment's worry of their future. I belonged to neither group. Only an instinct motivated me, and it was leading me nowhere.

It was this sense of being in a no man's land that led me to read books in the way I did. The enjoyment of a story was of

72

secondary importance. My solemn purpose was to cull advice from authors of worldly experience, or to discover reflections of my own moods which hitherto I had been unable to put into words. Hence I pored through the works of such writers as Turgenev, Dostoievsky, George Moore, Keyserling, Somerset Maugham, Proust and many others with a pencil in hand to mark a significant paragraph; and then later I would conscientiously copy it out into a notebook. In this way I became gradually aware that my moments of puzzlement and despair were not unique; and I even discovered it could be an advantage to be introspectively depressed. It developed one's understanding of other people.

The deb dances were over and the social games had moved to Cowes. There was nothing trivial to occupy my mind, and I spent my idle August days meandering along the Kings Road, or lying on the grass in Hyde Park, or sitting stifled in my room at Joubert Studios. Months of waiting and nothing had materialised. Nor was I any wiser than when I left Unilever as to what I was expecting. Just a Micawber instinct, and I knew I could not pursue it much longer.

Then one morning I received a pound note from my father and with it came a message: 'Keep your pecker up. It's going to be alright soon.' And so it was. That lunch time I called in at the Six Bells in the Kings Road. Some people I knew were there, and one of them introduced me to a pretty girl; and while I spent my pound note I learnt from her that she had a boy friend who was closely acquainted with Max Aitken, son of Lord Beaverbrook. By closing time she had promised to introduce me to her boy-friend. Within a fortnight I had been ushered into Max Aitken's office in the *Daily Express* building in Fleet Street. Within another fortnight I was in Manchester.

I had been given a month's trial as a *Daily Express* reporter.

SEVEN

I was away from London for eighteen months; and when I came back I wore a brown trilby hat jauntily aslant to my eyes, and I dangled a cigarette out of the corner of my mouth. I had begun my trial period in Manchester as an assistant to the night news reporter, roaming round Manchester until half past four in the morning, calling at hospitals and police stations, keeping in touch with fire brigades, seeking news of casualties and crime and fires. On my second night I was in Ancoats Hospital when an ambulance brought in a man who had been found dead in the street; nothing unusual about that, just one of several incidents during the year. The dour, kind, blunt Yorkshireman, the chief night news reporter, offered me the chance to write up the facts. My first story. A man found dead in the street ... but could I write it? The permutations of such a story were innumerable, and I tried them all. Five lines were required, yet I found it impossible to discover the magic formula; until at last ...

> Charles Kemp, aged eighty-five, of
> Garden Street, Ardwick, Manchester
> collapsed in the street late last
> night, and on being taken to Ancoats
> Hospital was found to be dead.

I was launched as a reporter.

I was soon aware, however, that my presence in the *Express* office was an embarrassment. My colleagues were friendly and helpful from the beginning, but I sensed the management considered me an inexperienced young Londoner who

74

had been foisted upon them against their will; and the sooner my month was up the better. I can be deceptive when I am on the defensive. Outwardly I am inclined to court trivial favours. I seek smiles from those with power over me, soothing myself that smiles are acts of approval. And yet there is another part of me which judges such fawning for what it is worth. I fawned on this occasion, expressing obsequious good mornings or good evenings when I came within voice distance of the powers that be; and yet all the while there was this other part of me, plotting hard. They could not turn me away if I produced enough stories which were published in the paper. I would make sure that I did so.

I had, however, a set-back within a week. Another young man was foisted on the management, a Cambridge graduate called Ronald Hyde; and when I learnt that his sponsor was the great Lord Beaverbrook himself, I felt despair. Neither of us was wanted, but if there were to be a choice it was obvious that Beaverbrook's protégé would be preferred; and so I looked across the room from where I sat at my typewriter and watched Hyde with disquiet. Then three days later there was no sign of Hyde in the office and I heard murmurings about a party the night before, and conclusions were drawn; and I was overjoyed. A black mark against my rival, for certain. If a man was prevented from arriving at the office by a hangover, surely he must be considered unreliable; and I felt a little more secure. But I had much to learn about the ways of newspaper offices, for a few days later Hyde had a story on the feature page with his name at the end of it. His name in print! Injustice! Why should he receive such an honour? I was in a panic, for suddenly it dawned on me that I would soon be out of a job, and I would be creeping back to London into a vacuum. For six weeks I lived with this terror, and then the magical moment arrived when we were both taken on. And soon we were to become close friends, and years later we shared a house in Richmond, and it was from this house that I married Jeannie. And Ronald himself became the most famous news editor of his time.

I learnt during my period in Manchester that tolerance is one of the main virtues. There was an extraordinary naturalness among the reporters, and if one of us were having a lean time, out of luck, stories going astray, the others would always try to help. There was not a single occasion, except the one created by myself, that anyone was jealous of another; and so my belief that careerists have to spend their lives trying to score points over each other was put in temporary suspense. I knew after a few weeks, for instance, that I could commit any foolishness without having to fear that someone might take advantage of it. There was a quiet friendliness among everyone, and I was happier than I had ever been in my life. I believed that I had found, in the newspaper profession, a kindly camaraderie which was unique.

I was also introduced into the gusto of living, and discovered to what extent I had lived in the shallows. I had been so sheltered that I had never been aware of sadness. My life had been a kind of minuet, an absorption in frivolous details; but now I began to become aware of humanity which hitherto had been only a word. There was a realisation that nobility of mind and action is usually secret, belonging to ordinary people who accept the good and the bad with fatalism. These obvious truths were to me at the time a revelation. It was as if I had spent my life in a cell, and I at last had been set free; and naturally I was bewildered by what I found.

I was enriched by these discoveries, but not enough to check my personal ambition. I observed, that's all. I was anxious to show sympathy, but only on terms that did not interfere with my work. News editors have no use for the fainthearted, and so ruthlessness was an essential if I were to keep my job. Yet I found I had also a ruthlessness of my own making. I loved the chase. I would rush out from the *Express* building in Ancoats Street on some story and I would have the same pent-up excitement of the huntsman after the fox. This was the mood of youth, the untarnished enthusiasm of inexperience, the reason why the young are chosen for tough jobs, the reason why the not so young are promoted, and the middle aged discarded.

Sometimes I had to do jobs which had no meaning except to satisfy the sadism of a newspaper's circulation, and then I had no alternative but to pretend to myself that I was being clever, an elaborate self-deception like someone who believes that otter hunting is useful. Acquiring photographs, for instance. There was little sense of achievement conning someone to give you a photograph, some personal photograph kept in a frame, so as to prove that I was better at conning than a rival.

'I am very very sorry,' I would say in a sepulchral voice, 'your little son David was run over by a bus this afternoon . . .'

'I know, I know . . .'

'Could I have a photograph of David? His little friends will be glad to see it in the paper.'

And because the mother was helpless, and off guard, she would hand me the photograph off the mantelpiece; and already I could see the gleam in the eye of my news editor when I handed it to him.

'You will have it returned tomorrow,' I would say, thanking her profusely, backing away from her tears to the door.

The art of a news reporter is to learn how to lull a victim, because all good reporters are confidence tricksters in embryo. The brash approach is only of value when the victim is highly excited, part of a drama upon which he has had no time to reflect; and then the reporter has only to ask the right questions for him to collect the facts of the story. The subtle story, which has to be dug out of the victim, relies on the same kind of intuition as that of a centre three quarter when he swerves through a mass of oppoents to score a try. There are rules to obey, but intuition brings the success. I was shown an example of this soon after I arrived in Manchester when I accompanied a senior colleague on a murder story. He interviewed several people during the day, and each time I grew restless and embarrassed by the idiotic questions he asked. They were so obvious, so inane, that I kept saying to myself that he must be the worst reporter in the office. At last I had to show my innocence.

'Why waste your time with such questions?'

He grinned at me.

'To make them think I'm as stupid as you think I am.'

I soon showed I had learnt my lesson. News came into the office that a missionary whose home was in Didsbury had been captured by bandits in central China and was being held to ransom; and I was sent off to Didsbury to interview the man's parents. When I arrived I found a posse of reporters already there, standing in a group outside the house. The door was shut, the curtains drawn, and I was told by my rivals that the parents were refusing to see anyone.

I guessed, however, that my rivals would soon drift away back to their offices, bored by the apparent uselessness of their wait; and so I went off for a walk. Then after an hour I came back, and strolled the few steps through the garden and knocked at the door. I was alone. No one was watching me as I waited for an answer. A man's voice asked who was there

'I've come to offer my sympathy,' I called back through

the closed door, 'I read about it in the evening paper.'

The door was inched open. 'Did you know Rudolph?'

I saw now it was an old man, and behind him, peering, was an old woman. A meek couple.

'I did not know him but I admired what he was doing.'

I was sitting in their kitchen with a cup of tea in my hand before I told them I was a reporter; and by that time I was so involved in their distress that they did not remember they had told my rivals to go away. I was mouthing sympathy, and listening, and they were relieved.

'Let's pray for his safety,' I said, and then the old man fetched a Bible, and the three of us knelt, and prayers were said.

Next day I wrote in my diary: 'Praise all round for me today for my missionary scoop. But does it mean I'm losing my soul? To my horror, as I poured out my sympathy, I found I was only thinking of the headlines I might get . . . *all I wanted was the story.*'

I consoled myself that if one remained conscious of one's hardness, the damage need not be too serious; as if the knowledge that it was wrong to knock someone over the head with a hammer was enough for the jury to bring in a verdict of not guilty. And yet, if the truth be told, nine times out of ten no one was hurt when a story was told against the initial wishes of the victim. Fury at first, but flattery from the notoriety often came afterwards. It was when a newspaper exposed a personal secret that the damage was done, and the hurt came to the innocent. Nonetheless, conning breeds a conscience though it may take some time to mature, and I had a long way to go.

Often, however, there were antidotes to tough reporting and I would be involved in some incident that moved me deeply. I was sent off to interview a man who had a painting in a local exhibition in Salford, and the point of the story

79

was that the man was a chronic invalid. I found him in a dingy Salford street, in a grim little house with a broken pane in the window of the front room. His wife was large and bossy, her hair straggling over her forehead, a dirty blouse, and she looked to me as if she had permanently lost patience with life. He was emaciated, jumpy, and as he breathed there was a sound like ancient bellows. He had been gassed in the First World War, and had been told he would never be able to lead a normal life again. They had been married a week before he had gone to the front.

I stood there asking him questions, and although he fidgeted and was nervous and looked like a scarecrow and his wife interrupted him, he gradually passed on to me an extraordinary sense of peace. I ceased to hear the traffic outside, lost my awareness of the poverty of the house, forgot the sharpness of my reporter role. He was pouring forth to me about the ideals he had when he was a young man, of how he had tried to keep true to them, and how, despite his inexperience of painting, he had endeavoured to put the lessons of his life on the canvas which was now hanging in the local exhibition. Its title had a melodramatic Victorian air about it, easy to smile at. He had called it Courage and Despair ... two men representing despair, a third who symbolised triumph over evil. A crude picture, perhaps, but it had its truth.

My home in Manchester was at 56 Portsmouth Street, off Ackers Street where the theatrical touring companies used to have their lodgings. I had stayed my first few days in a house in Ackers Street, arriving there on a wet Sunday night after calling from door to door looking for a room; and with my journalistic future beginning on the morrow. I had been seen off at Euston by my brother Colin, my mother and two or three others including Stephen Watts, then a famous film journalist. I had met Stephen Watts while I was at Unilever, and one day I asked him to dinner to seek his advice on my search for a journalistic career. He, however, misunderstood my invitation. He arrived, consumed the dinner uncomplainingly, and only months later did he tell me it was his second dinner of the evening. When I was appointed to Manchester, he took the trouble to tell me the rudiments of a reporter's life, and he came to Euston to wish me luck. And so there I was that evening, the rain pelting down on Manchester, a landlady who appeared immediately suspicious of me, remembering nostalgically the party which had seen me off, scared stiff of the future, and trying to console myself by playing a tune called My Dancing Lady on a portable record player.

Within a few days I was as suspicious of my landlady as she was of me, and I moved out and found a home with timid Miss Robinson in Portsmouth Street where I was to be happy all through my time in Manchester. It was a little street with little houses, and Miss Robinson was a little woman. She was also the ideal landlady, and I paid her £1 a week for a sitting room and bedroom including breakfast; and when I didn't have breakfast she took 6d off, and when I was away for the night she took 9d off. The place was scrupulously clean, and she darned my socks and mended my clothes, was always anxious to please, and never objected to the gaiety of my companions when they remained late at night in my sitting room.

My companions were usually from the shows which came to Manchester on their way to London; and I loved and laughed with a succession of chorus girls from Cochran and Charlot revues; and got into debt because of them. One unwise evening, after a Charlot first night, I invited a party to the Midland Hotel where the stars of the show were having their parties. 'Magnums!' cried the girls in Gaiety Girl fashion when I asked them what they would have to drink. 'Oysters!' they cried again when they looked at the menu. I remembered the party with distress while, for months afterwards, I paid off the bill in instalments. My salary was £3 a week.

There were others I first met in Manchester who, if I were to meet them again, I feel would be the same friends as in the beginning. Dickie Murdoch with off-beat humour but compelled by André Charlot to be a romantic, singing sentimental songs in a croaky voice, dancing like Jack Buchanan with shuffling steps; and speaking kindly of everyone. John Buckmaster, marvellously good looking, a golden boy, full of original talent, adored by the chorus, and so quiet. James Mason touring with a play of his own production, dry humour, ambitious, laconic and who, years later after Jeannie and I came together, was to taunt me for being an anti-cat man when Jeannie was urging me to have one. Norman Hackforth, voice of Twenty Questions, whom I envied because he won girls by his exquisite piano playing. Clifford Evans whom I still see. Giles Playfair, then working for Imperial Chemicals, who told me how he had been offered £50 if he could get every national newspaper to mention potatoes on one and the same day. He went off to Oxford and arranged that an article should appear in Cherwell saying that the Oxford boat race crew required more potatoes if they were to win. The article appeared and there were headlines in the newspapers: Potatoes to Pull. He won his £50.

This flirting with the fringes of show business suited both the flippant side of my nature and also my news editor; and I was soon being ordered to interview celebrities who, outwardly confident, were, I found, scared of the impending reaction of their north country audience. The pattern was usually the same; the suave arrival of the impresario and the chief performers, then interviews during which a studied effort was made to avoid condescension towards the reporters; then rumours that the scenery would not be ready in time for the show's opening, then emotional jollification at a party after the first night, then disappointment with the reviews, then rumours of backer withdrawals and new backer arrivals, feuds between stars, anxiety among the lesser fry, more rumours that there was no London theatre available; and then finally after a fortnight the caravanserai would depart; and the Mancunians would blasily wait for the next lot.

Under these conditions I met for the first time many of those whom I was to know for the rest of their lives. Noel Coward, when I first interviewed him, had just completed playing a part in a movie called *The Scoundrel*. He had never been in one before and I asked him his reactions.

'It's terribly, terribly monotonous,' he replied in his clipped fashion, 'acting all day in front of a tired electrician . . . and a lamp.'

C. B. Cochran and André Charlot were the showmen of the day, and they could charm anyone into liking them. They both had exquisite taste and a panache for the subtle things of life . . . Cochran with his spectacular revues, Charlot with his intimate ones; and they both had an inability to keep any money in the bank for themselves. The first time I met Cochran, the legendary Mistinguet was about to arrive in his suite at the Midland Hotel. 'Look out,' he said, 'she may be over seventy but she'll think she's your age when she sees you.'

I was to know André Charlot best, or Guv as everyone called him, when years later I was in Hollywood. He had lost so much money on his shows in England that he thought he might begin a new career in California; and that the movie people would wish to draw on his experience which had discovered such stars as Gertrude Lawrence, Bea Lillie,

Ronald Colman, Jessie Matthews and a host of others. They didn't; and when I was there he was living a parsimonious life in a small flat on the outskirts of Hollywood and refusing ever to leave it. 'After all,' he said in his charming French accent, 'a producer might call, and if I were out . . . well . . . he would forget to call me again.'

Many show people came and went and I would present myself to interview them. I remember John Gielgud saying. 'I'll never rest until I play the Prince Consort on the stage.' He has never done so. And I remember Constant Lambert, the lyrical composer of the Rio Grande, the conductor of the first English ballet company which ever made a profit, one of the most fascinating young musicians of the time who died before this remark of his came true. I made a note of it in my diary: 'There's a young girl in our company whom we are keeping back until she is ready. She is only sixteen and her name is Margot Fonteyn. She is going to be the greatest ballerina of all time.'

I became alive in Manchester; and I loved the wet dreary streets and the rattle of trams, the good fellowship in rumbustious pubs and the gaiety of my colleagues; and the excitement of being part of a far wider world than I had ever known before. I began to learn to judge people for what they were worth and not for what they appeared to be; and my role of reporter, however harsh and trivial the missions could sometimes be, had begun to teach me that all men are not born equal; and, like racehorses, they cannot all win.

I was always happy in Manchester, and I realised that I would never again enjoy the same undergraduate spirit of freedom. Yet I could not smother the urge to go forward. Manchester had awakened my senses, but London was where I belonged.

EIGHT

'Go round the world before you're thirty,' was the parting advice of my Manchester editor as he bade me good-bye and wished me luck. 'The opportunity will come . . . seize it.' The kind of advice people give when their own hopes have been disappointed, and I noted it in my diary, and wondered what the opportunity would be like when it came; and whether it would come in time because Hitler was shrieking at Nuremberg, and the civil war in Spain had begun, and fathers like my own had begun to worry about their sons.

I was now a reporter on the *Sunday Referee*. The paper had a reputation in its time but it was slowly tottering towards its end. The offices were in Tudor Street off Fleet Street, and they resembled a rabbit warren. The reporters' room was a hole which had no windows, where electric light had to blaze all day; and there was no library of reference books or files of newspaper cuttings like those available in Manchester, and the furniture was in need of repair. I was being paid three guineas a week retaining fee, and extra for each story published, the size of payment being related to the importance of the story.

I quickly found that the atmosphere was different from what I had known in Manchester where we trusted each other, and were pleased at each other's successes, and saw no reason why we should fear one another. There was instead an invisible irritant at work around me as I sat at my desk. My colleagues were pleasant enough but they seemed strained and reserved, and I did not feel comfortable. There was, of course, rivalry for the space obtained for each story but normally this would not have affected me. I was therefore annoyed with myself for feeling pleased when I had done better than a rival; and I was annoyed again when I thought my rivals were pleased by a failure of my own. I was, in fact, as I realised later, having my first experience of the jungle; the subtle eroding of the wish to trust, the gradual awareness of the need to be on guard in casual conversation, the avoidance of too much enthusiasm, the veneer of charm and gaiety and goodwill which momentarily deceives, the tension created by the sudden changing moods of the hierarchy, the surprising promotions or dismissals. All this was new to me, and so I remember with backhanded gratitude the time I spent in Tudor Street; for it gave me a warning.

I did not in the beginning pay much heed to my disquiet, because I had the joy of living in London again; and London then was unselfconscious. There was no need to strive for effect, no need to rely on gimmick publicity. London was the centre of the greatest force for peace the world had ever known, and she knew it, and she was lazily insolent in taking it for granted that everyone knew it too. Small things made me happy; a fourpenny ride on the open deck of a number 14 bus through Fulham and the West End and further; five bob spent on an evening out in a pub, yet money enough for a hangover next day; listening to the fussy hoots of the tugs on the river or watching the Changing of the Guard because it was a routine and not a tourist attraction; sandwiches with a girl in the early morning at the coffee stall in Sloane Square; leaving front doors open without thought of theft; a safe stroll in the park on a warm summer's night; Queen Mary in her toque; a silent sky. Yet the pace of living at the time seemed fast enough. There were nervous breakdowns, and drug addicts, and people who tried to get away from it all, and morals didn't stop a girl from going to bed with a man if she wanted to. The base doesn't change very much.

I stayed at first with my father and mother who had rented a furnished house for a few weeks in Elm Park Gardens in Chelsea, a high storey house of endless stairs; and I used to hurry back to them from my unsettled kind of day, and climb the stairs to my room, and say to myself that although I loved my parents their normality did not fit in with my unreliability, and I wished I was on my own. I did not have to tell my mother this in words and, without saying anything to me, she began to look for a flat for me. And one evening, after I had arrived home late for dinner, irritable because I had left friends enjoying themselves, she broke the news that she had found for me the ideal flat.

It was not a flat. It was a mews cottage . . . and it *was* ideal. It was off Elm Park Road and between The Vale and Beaufort Gardens both leading to the Kings Road, and the address was 20 Elm Park Garden Mews, and you came to it after passing under a brick archway which seemed to have no reason for being there. It was a little street which ran towards the Fulham Road, and at the beginning of my living there it was a working street with chauffeurs coming and going in limousines; and these were always being washed and polished and tinkered with while children played noisily around watching their fathers in overalls, and watching them again in peaked caps and dark uniforms as they drove from the mews on the way to their dignified assignments. Then as people like myself moved in, and others who remodelled the cottages in fancy ways, the mood of the mews changed and the chauffeurs who remained became the odd men out; and there came a day when the authorities no longer considered it a mews and they changed the name to Elm Park Lane.

The front door of the mews cottage opened on a tiny stairway and this led straight up into the sitting-room which had a wooden balustrade, like that of a minstrel's gallery, overlooking the stairway. There was a bedroom, a kitchen,

87

and a bathroom like a boxroom because it had no windows. Beneath the sitting room was a garage, and on the left of the front door was a ground floor spare room which was to be used by my brother Nigel when he came to London on visits from where he lived in Hertfordshire. The place was unfurnished and dilapidated but my mother, while I worked, supervised the decorating and went bargain hunting for furniture. I still have some of the furniture; the sofa is at Minack, and the kitchen cupboard which came from Peter Jones is in the barn behind a pile of fertiliser bags; and its contents are now nuts and bolts, and half used tins of paint. So the day came when I moved into the first home of my own, and I realised it was another of the original pleasures, and I felt I could conquer the world.

A limited world, however. I was only wishing to enjoy myself, and this meant spreading my contacts, and building up my ego, and living for the day. I rejoiced, therefore, when I was sent to interview famous people, or found myself on a murder story having a drink with the suspected murderer, or sitting in the hotel room of a young aristocrat who was believed to be the brains behind a jewel robbery, or commiserating with the parents of an eloping daughter. It exhilarated me to watch from the outside how other people behaved when assuaging vanity or avoiding danger.

One day my editor, R. J. Minney who was to become successful in wider fields than journalism, sent me to interview the legendary William Randolph Hearst who had arrived at Claridges with his friend, the famous Marion Davies. They were on their way to St Donat's Castle in Wales which Hearst had bought on a whim and had stuffed with some of the treasures it was his habit to collect. I was naturally a little apprehensive over interviewing the most powerful newspaper owner the United States has ever known, but I also thought it might be useful . . . one day I hoped to be going to America and if I pleased Mr Hearst many doors might be opened.

I found him sitting in a chair too small for him, heavy jowled and pouch-eyed, wearing a tweedy grey suit the jacket of which hung floppily around a waistcoat which was crumpled in folds. He reminded me of Toad when Toad was about to boast, except there was a wariness in Mr Hearst's eyes that Toad never had. I posed questions to him about his anti-British newspapers and the reason for this, and why it was he still liked to have a home in Britain. He replied, as owners of newspaper chains are inclined to reply, that he exercised no control over his editors; and that he harboured no ill feelings towards the British and so it was only a coincidence that his newspapers were so inclined to attack us. I asked him also about his art collecting . . . and at this moment I realised that within a couple of feet of my face was a winning Marion Davies offering me peanuts from a plate. Inexperienced though I was, I sensed conflict. I turned from Mr Hearst in his chair, and asked questions of Miss Davies instead. All the old questions.

'Which part did you like playing most?'

'Who is your favourite director?'

'Is there any part which you want specially to play?'

Old Mr Hearst sat solidly in his chair while Marion Davies played her charm on me; and when I left, she followed me into the Claridges corridor and said:

'The old man,' and a thumb went over her shoulder towards the suite, 'has been getting all the publicity this trip. *Could* you do a story about me?' And the limpid blue eyes had tears in them.

There was a curious sequel. I returned to the office and wrote one story about Miss Davies, the other about Mr Hearst. The first was a casualty of the sub-editors and did not appear in the Sunday issue. The second was given some prominence. I thought no more of it until my editor on the following Tuesday handed me a telegram addressed to him from St Donat's. It read: 'Deny ever having seen your reporter. Signed William Randolph Hearst.' No letter followed, no explanation; and my editor was as baffled as I was.

I sometimes had an unfortunate tendency to miss out the most important questions when interviewing someone, and I would realise my forgetfulness as soon as I had left. Usually I would return, ask the questions and all would be well; but there were occasions when the subject had been thankful to see the back of me the first time, and so I was barred from seeing him again.

I had arrived for instance on a Saturday morning in Belfast by the overnight boat with the aim of interviewing von Ribbentrop, then German Foreign Minister, who was staying the weekend with Lord Londonderry. It was a time when the latter was considered to be excessively pro-German and I had been instructed that an interview with him would be a good second best to an interview with Ribbentrop. I had a firm belief, however, as I set out in a taxi to the Londonderry mansion that neither would be willing to see me; and I was right.

I stopped the taxi at a kiosk near the estate and rang up, explaining that I had come over from London specially, etc. etc. . . . and after an interval while the message was relayed to Lord Londonderry, I was abruptly told I was wasting my time. Thereupon I told the taxi to drive to the front door where I was told to my face that I was not wanted. I was thoroughly dispirited because I knew my newspaper would not look kindly at the expenses of my journey if the result was total failure. I *had* to see one of them. My taxi driver now came to my help, for he informed me that he knew of a hole in the wall of the estate which was close to the kitchen garden; and the kitchen garden was not far from the back door of the mansion. It was his suggestion that I should enter through the back door unannounced, then find my way inside to Lord Londonderry's quarters. It was risky but I had to try something, and so the taxi driver drove me to the hole in the wall, and within a minute I was alone in the kitchen garden.

I walked up a path with herbs growing as a border, past an old-fashioned greenhouse, then right along another path which led straight to the backdoor. I didn't see a soul. I now walked boldly inside, turned left because I sensed that this was the direction to the living-room, and then had a fright. A man was coming towards me. He came straight along the passage, went past me without a word, and disappeared.

I was now highly excited by my adventure. I walked on a few yards, came to an open door, went through it into a hall, and there I found myself being stared at by several Londonderrys who were hanging on the walls. And at the same moment I saw the real, live Londonderry through another doorway, and with Ribbentrop beside him. They were staring out through the french windows into the garden.

I coughed.

'Excuse me, sir . . .'

Had Lord Londonderry displayed surprise, annoyance or just plain anger, I feel sure my mind would have reacted with speed. Instead, while Ribbentrop turned a lazy smile on me Lord Londonderry with utmost charm ignored my break-in and asked me what I wanted. I once again explained, and thereupon he gave me an innocuous statement which he told me I could quote; and I was so thankful that there was *something* I could report back to my editor that my nerve, which had carried me so far, promptly collapsed. It was only half an hour later as the taxi was speeding me back to Belfast that I realised I had been a fool. I had achieved the hardest part of my task by succeeding in seeing them. So why hadn't I asked any questions?

Schiaparelli was the Balmain of the late thirties. I had ghosted an article for her on the general subject of her life; and when it was suggested to her that she wrote a series of articles enlightening English women how they should dress, disclosing the fashionable secrets of a Parisienne and all those beguiling charms expected of the French, she agreed to do so on the condition that once again I was her 'ghost'. I was flattered, and I also thought what a useful education it would be for me. And when she further proposed that I should go to Paris every month to gather the material for each set of articles, I had expectations that I would be launched into a world of exquisite models and elegantly conducted affairs.

Schiaparelli had recently opened a branch of her House in London and the articles, therefore, were a means to advertise the branch without cost to herself; but she was not going to allow me to mix business with pleasure. Thus the first visit to see her, my first ever visit to Paris, set the tone for the others. I sat in her office overlooking the Place Vendôme, notebook in hand, watching her aquiline features and listening to her voice as it tattooed her views on the ways a woman can captivate a man. 'Accessories, these are important.' (She had recently opened a boutique of accessories.) 'Scarves . . . a gay scarf transforms a plain woman.' And so on. I still, however, had hopes that when the interview was over she would propose introducing me to the Paris of the gay Parisienne so that I would be able to taste the flavours of what I was writing about. Alas no. She introduced me instead to an elderly American publicity woman. We had dinner alone.

My pursuit of pleasure was aided by my being at times a

cabaret columnist, a radio columnist, a theatrical columnist, and a disc columnist. None of my columns had any influence because no one took the *Sunday Referee* very seriously, but they provided opportunities which would otherwise have been denied me. Discs, for instance, came to 20, Elm Park Lane from the recording companies in large packages; the cabaret column meant I was showered with invitations from night clubs and restaurants; the radio and theatrical columns enabled me to arrange a meeting with any girl I might admire from afar.

I had, for instance, loved a sloe-eyed film star called Sylvia Sydney; and there had been an occasion after seeing her in Elmer Rice's *Street Scene* at the Empire Theatre in Leicester Square when I had walked home praying for a miracle that the next girl I met would be her. In due course she did in fact come to London and when I saw that she was staying at Claridge's I realised the long awaited miracle could now come true. I rang up and asked to interview her.

She was as nervous as I was, this girl whom I had watched conquer Clark Gable, Burgess Meredith and other highly paid lovers. And this gave me momentary confidence, and I asked her to come out to dinner with me, and when she said yes, I guessed I would be wise if I took her somewhere away from the conventional restaurants if I were to make an impression on her; and so there we were at Quo Vadis with Leoni hovering around us, a lighted table lamp between us, and I with a feeling of unreality that I should be so close to this girl I had worshipped from my cinema seat. I had no car of my own, and I had borrowed one from a friend, a Baby Austin which was even smaller than a Mini; and after dinner I told her I would take her to the most beautiful view in London. This was the floodlit Battersea Power Station, the first floodlit building in London, and we stood on the Embankment on the opposite side of the river and watched in silence the white plumes of smoke disappearing into the night; and, long afterwards, she told an American journalist in an interview that it was her most memorable sight in London. Perhaps it was. As for me the tension of the evening had been too great. I was out of my depth. I had only admiration to offer and she had plenty of that; and I never dared ask to see her again.

This initiative I displayed, superficial though its intention may have been, did on occasions bring me a special reward. There was a girl called Jan, for instance. She was playing a part at the Criterion Theatre when I first saw her, and Twentieth Century Fox had just offered her a contract in Hollywood, and so I made this the excuse to interview her. She had recently come from Melbourne with her mother, and she was slim and dark with blue eyes, and highly intelligent; and there was a calmness about her which balanced my own frivolous exuberance. Sometimes people come together and remain content with each other for a while because their personal circumstances by luck coincide. Soon their friends take it for granted that they are always together, and neither is invited anywhere without the other. It is a soothing time; and yet both inwardly know they are living in a kind of suspense account. They do not belong to each other. They suit each other for the time being, that's all. They are waiting. Thus it was with Jan and me.

Jan was only in Hollywood for a few months, and one evening after her return I was telling her that Godfrey Winn was leaving the *Daily Mirror* and the column which he had made so famous. And I added: 'How I pity the man who succeeds him!' Godfrey Winn, of course, had won his fame by his courage, by being blatantly sincere, and by setting out to help his readers in a way that no columnist had tried to do before. His success and popularity was such that anyone who

94

succeeded him could only be a pale carbon copy; and so hence my expression of pity.

The very next morning I had a telephone call from an executive of the *Daily Mirror* asking me to meet him in El Vino's, the Fleet Street wine bar. I had left the *Sunday Referee* and was now working on the *Sunday Express* where John Gordon was editor. I was also writing occasional magazine articles and one of these, a lighthearted piece on my likes and dislikes, had caught the attention of the *Mirror*. I had no clue of this when I arrived at El Vino's and found the executive in an alcove with a bottle of champagne on the table in front of him. I had no clue that half an hour later I would be leaving El Vino's as Godfrey Winn's successor.

The transformation in my life was immediate and startling; and I joined the procession of unknowns who become overnight stars because it is good business for somebody else. Within a month I had bought myself an elegant Buick, received numerous flattering invitations from people I had never met, and gazed at a hoarding in Trafalgar Square which hailed 'the brilliant young writer Derek Tangye' who was currently denouncing hypocrisy in his articles in the *Daily Mirror*. There were also posters on buses with earnest photographs of myself staring down at the traffic. My father, fascinated by these, would stand for hours with a camera, waiting for buses which halted long enough for him to photograph the extraordinary claims concerning his son: 'Derek Tangye exposes this,' 'Derek Tangye condemns that.' Nothing so peculiar had ever happened to a member of the family before. As for myself I realised I had become a celebrity without justification, but this did not prevent me enjoying the situation. The first taste of success, however tenuous, is always sweet.

But quite soon I received a warning to keep my ebullience under control; a witty comment from Cyril Connolly who lived five minutes away from 20 Elm Park Lane in a flat at the corner of The Vale and Kings Road.

I had met him first when I went with my father and mother for a holiday at Dulverton in Devonshire. We stayed at a hotel called the Caernarvon Arms and the object of the holiday was the trout fishing; and this my father and I did for most of each day. Indeed most of the solid looking guests were trout fishermen and the subject of conversation was inevitably limited to the trout which got away or the trout which was caught. In this setting the presence of Cyril Connolly was incongruous, more especially because he and his wife Jean were accompanied wherever they went by a marmoset. The other guests clearly did not approve of such unusual behaviour, and my father and mother called it absurd exhibitionism. I, on the other hand, was fascinated by this gesture against convention. It had an aura of intellectual bohemianism which caught my imagination. Not that I knew then who Cyril Connolly might be. He had still to write *The Rock Pool*. I had still to read and reread *The Unquiet Grave* which lies on my desk as I write.

I did not meet him again for some years, but when he came to live in the Kings Road there began a period when I saw him often. He was kind, and delightful, and witty. And I burst into his flat one day and told him about some graphic incident connected with my column. He sat tubbily in a chair listening to me, mischief in his eyes warning me of what might be coming, saying not a word until the appropriate pause occurred when he could deflate me. Then:

'Derek,' he said, mockingly solemn, 'you're selling your soul for a penny a day.'

Outwardly, I am sure, I appeared to be doing just that. I was rushing around too much, going to too many parties and theatre first nights, accepting too easily the praise of people who wanted to make use of my column; and generally behaving as if success had gone to my head. My behaviour, however, was in fact a nervous reaction. As the days went by I began to realise the extraordinary responsibility my column entailed. It was not a satirical column or a column which could win easy applause by knocking some public figure off his perch. It was a column which reached people who were too ordinary to be cynical and too close to the sadness of life to be insincere. Such people needed a focus in life; and Godfrey Winn had discovered this and the *Daily Mirror* had exploited it.

There was, therefore, another role for me to play; and it made me feel inadequate and humble. As a reporter I had had plenty of experience of nosing my way into the private affairs of people suffering from misfortune, but I had remained an outsider. I was now, however, embroiled. I had the usual numerous letters asking for advice, and I would try to answer them without my words sounding too remote; and people would visit me and tell me stories which were true but which were difficult to believe.

Then there was the Fund which Godfrey Winn had launched one day in his column, and which I now continued to operate. Its object was to help any reader in need, and when the Fund ran low I had only to write that more money was wanted, and the money would come rolling in. It was a salutary experience to discover how generous people could be, and equally salutary to discover the various ways in which I could dispense the money.

Lucid assessment of facts did not come into my calculation when I decided whether or not someone deserved help or not. I had to rely on instinct whether each case was genuine. I probably made many mistakes but, if there were such mistakes, they were compensated by the numerous times the Fund saved someone in a crisis. Such times were diverse in their nature. A city typist told me a long story how she had stolen the petty cash, and now full of con science wanted to replace it before she was found out; a mother who was dying from a lingering illness wanted to take her children to look at the sea for the first time in their lives; a father with a son in the condemned cell in Leeds Prison needed the money for his fare so that he could see his son before the execution. I faced dramas like these every day.

Meanwhile, outside this private world, the Spanish Civil War became bloodier, Chamberlain wooed Mussolini, Anthony Eden resigned in protest, Hitler seized Austria; and the very few tried to wake up the public into realising that World War II was on its way. But the old preferred to remember their nightmares, and the young to live their dreams, and nobody took any notice. It was cosier to be fatalistic. It was easier to let history be in command. We were prepared to read about war, become emotional about it, so long as we did not have to think about it.

For a while my column seemed to go well enough; and then I began to sense there were forces at work which aimed at dislodging me. Nothing unusual about this if you are in a job which other people would like, for it is part of the price you have to pay for holding it. I carried on as if nothing was happening and I would clatter through the day, then return to 20 Elm Park Lane and flop into bed exhausted . . . only to wake up at dawn with a nasty feeling that in any case I was not fitted to be a true success at the job. I was therefore agreeably surprised when one morning a senior member of the hierarchy called me into his office, told me he was pleased with my work, and that he proposed to lengthen my contract. Moreover he outlined a plan to me whereby I was to visit a European capital every weekend, beginning with a trip to Paris the following Friday. On the Friday I came into the office with my suitcase, my seat booked on the afternoon plane, when the man called me in again and told me of another idea. He politely informed me that the policy of the *Mirror* had been changed overnight, and my column wasn't wanted any more.

Jan was playing the young girl in Robert Sherwood's *Idiot's Delight* at the Globe Theatre. In those days producers were not usually interested in presenting plays which stirred the conscience, but the fabulous Henry Sherek, most imaginative of conventional producers, gambled his money because he believed the public ought to see it. He wanted the public to think about war. He wanted the public to wake up I loved the play myself and I used to go often to see it and listen to the sad, rasping voice of Raymond Massey who played Jan's father. It haunts me still.

I rang up Jan immediately after I had been fired from my column, and arranged to collect her after the theatre. I felt pleasantly calm about the situation. I suppose it was a relief that my forebodings had at last materialised, and I no longer had to pretend that all was well. Yet I was sensible enough to realise that I was in a fix. The over publicised kind of column I had been writing had no place in any other newspaper. Indeed the huge amount of publicity I had received was now a drawback. No other newspaper would want me. And I had a sudden chilly thought that I would have to creep back to being an anonymous reporter.

It was sometime during the afternoon that I had my brilliant idea. It had to be acted upon immediately. The secret of its whole success depended upon my securing the agreement of those who had fired me.

That night Jan and I went to the Berkeley, and we sat in a corner watching the dancers from a distance, and listening to Al Collins playing his violin. A waiter had filled our glasses with champagne.

'Well,' she asked, 'what happened?'

I gave her the details, then went on to explain the idea I had had.

'And they agreed,' I said, raising my glass, 'they're going to publish a column saying I'm resigning because I'm going round the world.'

'When will it appear?'

'I've written it . . . tomorrow.'

I had remembered the advice my Manchester editor had given me.

NINE

Algonquin,
West 44th Street,
New York.
June 29th, 1938.

Dear all of you,

How you'd laugh and laugh if you were with me. All my life I've heard of the beauty of the New York skyline; of the heat of New York's summer months; of the fuss they'll make of anyone on the celebrity fringe.

Well yesterday morning I was up at seven to watch us coming in ... we were due to dock at ten. And I thought of all the carefully organised publicity dope which was to launch me into the money-earning newspaper world, and I wanted to be wide awake and ready when the reporters arrived to see me.

But I was to have a series of surprises. To begin with the skyline was hidden by a drizzling mist as cold as any in England. Well, I said to myself, that doesn't matter because I'll be able to pay all my attention to the press.

They came aboard the *Aquitania* with the immigration officials and began rushing round asking questions of one person and another. There I was waiting expectantly and when nothing happened I went down to my cabin thinking they might be there. Then back on deck. They were interviewing all and sundry, but did they approach me? No indeed. Not the faintest notice was taken of me! Oh dear it was funny ... and then when I got to the Algonquin I hadn't been there an hour when the telephone rang and a man from some press agency asked if I would allow him to take my photograph. Ah, I thought, they have found me at last. Only later did I learn it was a trick ... all visitors are asked and vanity makes them agree. Then they sell the visitors the photographs!

I had lunch with the *Daily Mirror* man here. He told me I hadn't a cat in hell's chance of making any money on New York papers. So all the publicity handouts have produced a puff ball!

D

The Royalton,
44 West 44th Street,
New York.
July 10th.

Dear brothers,

I've moved from the Algonquin to this hotel across the street where I have a lovely room with bath at the top of the building and a skyline of Broadway skyscrapers for 15 dollars a week.

I went to Sing Sing yesterday. It overlooks the Hudson and has the atmosphere of a public school, prisoners black and white wandering around at will in grey flannel trousers and white shirts. The warder who took me round pointed out to me the most distinguished prisoners, and then I was literally forced to sit in the electric chair in the murderer's wing which I thought pretty poor taste. The warder just laughed.

D.

The Royalton,
44 West 44th Street,
New York.
August 1st.

Darlings,

Apparently two letters have gone astray and I gather from daddy's letter today that one of them was from dear Colin concerning the disastrous state of my finances at home. I thought the sale of the Buick would pay my debts. I have at the moment £44 which isn't bad and that will last for another six weeks but it means I can spend nothing except on food and gives me no chance to go places getting material for articles. For instance when I went to Sing Sing the fare was 2 dollars and to tip the warder was another 4 dollars. And it will be a long time before I'm paid for the article. However, all will be well, and I'm sorry to cause all this trouble.

D

The Royalton,
44 West 44th Street,
New York.
August 9th.

Darlings,

Colin's letter still has not arrived, and I still haven't the slightest idea about my finances except the gloomy remarks of yours like 'you can't walk on air' and 'what are you going to do?'

If it is as bad as you say there must be a mistake somewhere. Anyhow my reply to the news is to get as far away from England as possible, because I will do everything in my power to stop coming home before April next year. So I leave by Greyhound bus for San Francisco on Friday. The journey across America takes four nights and five days, but the price including food is only £10!

D.

Hotel Roosevelt,
Wabash Avenue,
Chicago.
August 14th.

My dears,

I started from New York on August 12th, 8.35 p.m. N.Y. time and got here last night after a hell of a battering in the bus with never a stop long enough for a wash or a shave. I start off again at lunch time for Salt Lake City where I'll stay a night or two and recover and do a story on the Mormons, then I go on to Reno. Part of the advantage of this bus trip is that I can stop over when I like, then take another bus.

D.

Sacramento.
August 22nd.

Dear all of you,

Next stop San Francisco! Meanwhile I'm sending you some notes I've made on the trip:

The woman whose head I brushed with my arm on the first night as I put on my coat. She was asleep in the seat beside me, and bellicosely as she awoke, she snapped: 'Did you hit me?' . . . 5.30 in the morning, a cafe in the Alleghany mountains sipping coffee with a gramophone blaring . . . the cloud of flies that filled the bus after Cleveland and the ferocious little man with flat ears and the eyes of Mussolini who spent his time wildly killing them, and who when we got to Chicago said: 'Watcha think of sharing a room? Cheaper you know' . . . 'So long folks,' said the drivers when they changed over every five hours . . . and the woman who kept her hat on all night . . . summer lightning above the plains of Iowa, grey, brown, black horses against the skyline standing head to head, flapping their tails because of the flies . . . non-stop quacking of the woman in the back of the bus. Just before Cheyenne she changed her place to one behind mine. I found she also smelt, so I got out and stayed the night . . . and it was the first time I'd seen cowboys in their full regalia. Everybody was drunk and I could get nothing out of anyone except slurred words . . . the little horror of a cowboy in the bar who was so proud of his belt. 'Yellow rat!' he cried, waving it in the air, 'you have to go far south to get that!' . . . there is a sign as you go into Reno: 'You can't do anything wrong here, we make it legal!' . . . I reached San Francisco with exactly ten cents left which wasn't enough to tip the porter who took my luggage up at the Pickwick Hotel . . . I feel rather depressed.

D.

956 Sacramento Street,
San Francisco.
September 9th.

Darlings,

The war news looks appalling and by the time you get this it may have begun. Even if it hasn't it is merely a question of time, a few months, a year. I am overcome by a sense of futility. If war does break I know I will come back. It would not be, as you know, from any raging desire to put on uniform but a quaint sense of loyalty to England. And yet am I right? Should one recognise one's country or get away from civilisation and live as an individual? Oh blast Hitler, hell to the man, as if there weren't worries enough when there's peace.

D

956 Sacramento Street,
San Francisco.
September 12th.

Darlings,

Since my last letter Hitler has spoken and sounds as if he's climbing down. It's damnable how he keeps the world on a see-saw. However, to brighter things.

'I've been having a wonderful time with Gertie Lawrence. She's playing here in *Susan And God*, and every night I go to one of her parties. Lack of funds of course has meant that I haven't been able to do entertaining in return, but the other evening I had a brilliant idea. I was in her dressing-room with some other people, and I breezily told them how I had lost all my money gambling at Reno. I spoke so convincingly that they believed me and thought it very funny. Now Gertie tells everyone and hoots of laughter follow, and I don't have to spend a dime.

One night we had a hilarious evening in Chinatown which the Chief of Police arranged for Gertie. She is the most enchanting person, scatterbrained and gay, but never missing a thing. We went all over the place escorted by detectives, had a wonderful dinner at a Chinese restaurant and when we were walking home early in the morning we found bang in the middle of Grant Avenue a couple of English sailors ... their ship H.M.S. *York* was in San Francisco on a courtesy visit. Up went Gertie gaily to one of them, because she – like me – felt homesick at the sight of them, and said: 'I am Gertie Lawrence!' The two men swayed, they were very drunk, then one of them murmured in reply: 'Well, sshow ush where we can get shome women.'

The play is moving on to Los Angeles and I will be seeing her when I get to Hollywood.

D.

Blackburn Apartments,
1805 N. Wilcox Avenue,
Hollywood.
September 26th.

Darlings,

This letter could be such a gay affair. There's so much laughter I

105

could tell you about. But I have just come from the corner of this street and Hollywood Boulevard where I've been standing outside a shop listening, while for an hour and a half the mad Mullah of Germany tore the world to pieces punctuated by the organised hysteria of his followers. By the time you get this letter the bombs may have already come but at least, instead of the sudden horde of death that H. G. Wells foretold would come in the night, the horde will be expected. Last week I thought Chamberlain had surrendered totally, and even now I can find no saving grace for the manner he has handled it. The Americans jeer at us and all sorts of rude remarks have been made to me. But it is easy for them. They're safe. I do pray you are all safe in Cornwall.

D.

Blackburn Apartments,
1805 N. Wilcox Avenue,
Hollywood.
October 2nd.

Dear all of you,
Quite unbelievable. Like you and everyone else I just didn't see how it could be avoided. Such a miracle happening once may mean it can happen again, but now the first excitement is over I have a foreboding. Yet at least a lot of people who would have been killed have another year to live. War will come, that's certain, and I hope to goodness the country will rearm like mad . . . and meanwhile *how* I'm going to enjoy myself.

D.

Blackburn Apartments,
1805 N. Wilcox Avenue,
Hollywood.
October 14th.

Darlings,
I'm having a glorious time and the £50 you sent me has made me feel like a millionaire. You've been wonderfully generous and I for my part haven't been wasting a cent. Do you know that since August 12th my average expenses a week have averaged only £7?

Of course I haven't done badly though it means no entertaining whatsoever. I've got a lovely apartment here which really costs £10 a week but the landlady is letting me have it for £3 as there are not many people about. The other apartments seem to be filled with ambitious mothers escorting hopeful daughters. The whole place is geared to celluloid and the mirage of its riches. Of course it is all very synthetic but it's prettier than I expected; I never for instance expected the Santa Monica mountains to be so close, and I've never known such mass beauty. You walk along Hollywood and Sunset Boulevards and pass one exquisite thing after another. Golden hair and dark hair, slim figures and tapering legs, and always youth.

I'm seeing a lot of Miles Mander and Guy Charlot. Miles has just played the visitor in Wuthering Heights with Merle Oberon and Laurence Olivier, they say he's marvellous. He's so charming and gay, and vague, and kind. We went out to see his friend, an old silent star Jameson Thomas whom you may remember, and who is dying of TB in a tiny clinic in the Sierra Madre. A tiny room too. And when Miles told him I'd come from England, this gaunt, very good looking Englishman kept murmuring from his bed: 'I'm dying to see England again.'

Guy Charlot is absolutely broke, but is so amusing about it. He laughs and laughs about my Reno gambling story, and I must say it is working just as well here as in San Francisco. He himself who has launched so many stars including of course Gertie, cannot now have a meal even at the Brown Derby. He just sits in his apartment, waiting for letters, and wonderfully dignified. We've been poring over maps together plotting my journey to Tahiti.

I saw Gertie several times while she was at the Biltmore in Los Angeles. Once after the show I was alone with her in the dressing room, and she was hoping Douglas Fairbanks would call. Minute after minute went by, and I became aware that I was an interloper, and yet also my presence helped to hide the fact the man hadn't called and wasn't going to call. I thought she was very sad. And then a lucky thing happened. Johnny Green suddenly arrived, the composer and pianist, whom Gertie had known since her Charlot days, and the three of us went off to a hotel where there was no one in the restaurant except a couple of morons, a piano and ourselves.

As soon as we had finished our supper, Johnny went over to the piano and started to play. Then the morons moved out and we were left alone, and I asked Gertie to sing Some Day I'll Find You and she answered that she always sang it out of tune and Nöel always laughingly complained. Then she sang it to the empty room. And of course I never knew that it was Johnny Green who composed Body and Soul. He brought it to Gertie with three other songs when he was very broke, and she bought a share in all the songs, then she sang Body and Soul on the BBC and also took it to Ambrose . . . well you know the result. So there I was that evening alone for an audience except for a waiter, listening to Gertie sing and Johnny Green play song after song until it was time to go home. Johnny Green is writing a musical for her, and she's thrilled because the show opens with her on a bicycle, pedalling furiously, with her bottom to the audience!

D.

Blackburn Apartments,
1805 N. Wilcox Avenue,
Hollywood.
November 2nd.

Dear Colin,

I couldn't believe it when I heard your voice just now. What a wonderful gesture to ring me, and now I feel I missed out everything I was going to say in excitement. Only three minutes when we're accustomed to talk for an hour when I'm home! Anyhow, you know my plans and that though I'll be on a shoestring I think I'll be able to carry them out. I'll board the *Nyhorn* at San Pedro the day after tomorrow and we're due in at Panama on the 15th. Then I go over to Cristobal to wait for the French boat for Tahiti and I'll go steerage which only costs about £10. I'll wander around the South Seas for a while then go on to New Zealand and Australia, and after that the Far East and home by the Trans-Siberian Express. Doesn't it sound marvellous? It was Miles Mander's idea that I should go on the Trans-Siberian . . . he says that if there's a war anyone who has just come from Japan across

108

Russia will be specially wanted. I've an extraordinary intuition that he's right.

D.

Hotel Washington,
Cristobal.
November 21st.

Dear all of you,

I sent a sheaf of notes off yesterday to you about my *Nyhorn* voyage. It was a fabulous saga. Now I'll be boarding the *Ville d'Amiens* for Papeete tomorrow, and I'll be thankful to get out of this place. The hotel is very ritzy but the town and that includes Colon is the filthiest, smelliest, hottest place I've ever been to. The only bright time I've had was when Tyrone Power flew in for a night. He had told me in Hollywood he would probably be there about the same time, and he called me as soon as he arrived, and we had a terrific evening touring the nightclubs. He is the nicest young American I have ever met, humorous, gay and sincere, and none of that flashy phoniness so many of them have. We finished up with a couple of girls, a bottle of whisky and a gramophone in his room at the hotel, but we hadn't been there twenty minutes when a manager told us the girls were not allowed. So the great lover had to take them home.

D

Ville d'Amiens.
December 4th.

Darlings,

Have just heard that there is a ship leaving Tahiti for Vancouver tomorrow and I'm going to rush something out to catch it. We get in at dawn tomorrow. We've had glorious weather since passing the equator. But thank heavens the journey is over as there is no privacy in the steerage and all the time I have an appalling gnawing feeling of hunger. We eat on tin plates which have always a greasy smell and so have the glasses while the water doesn't taste like water. The food is just what is left over from the second-class plates and I haven't touched meat since I got aboard because it is always high. The mattresses are of straw but that hasn't mattered. Sometimes I've slept on deck until the men washing the decks in the early morning have woken me up with the hose . . . but tomorrow it's all over and I pray it won't be raining, it's the rainy season, because I want my Tahiti dream to come true.

D.

P.S. – Have just arrived and am waiting to land. The arrival was beyond my wildest dreams. The sun rose as we arrived, and I wanted to shout and cry and pray for the beauty of it. The water was so still that it seemed solid, and the most wonderful scent brushed the air, hibiscus, the *tiare tahiti*, and all the luxuriant jungle of the island. I felt incoherent with happiness. As we slowly sailed towards Papeete I could see the weird outline of Moorea, then I saw a canoe with a white sail and a man naked but for his red pareu, and soon we reached the opening in the reef, and we turned to sail through it. Here at last was the land of Gauguin, Rupert Brooke, Maugham, Keable, here within my sight were the things they loved, and the tranquillity and happiness men dream about as they obey the conventions of civilisation. I feel I've found another dimension to my life.

D.

Papeari, Tahiti.
December 31st.

My dear brothers,

I am at the lonely end of Tahiti, the Presqu' Isle, in a bungalow built on stilts into the lagoon so that I hear the water lapping beneath me through the bamboo stilts, and through the bamboo which make up the walls I watch the moon and the stars. But it's not perfect because in a bungalow near me is an American who has a radio and who instead of being happy with the noises of the night, insists on listening to dance bands. Why do they always have to have their pleasures man made?

Otherwise I'm quite alone except for Mauu and his dozens of children. He is one of the characters of the South Seas. He is very

110

fat, always with a red pareu round his middle, and with breasts sagging like those of an old woman. He knew Rupert Brooke, and he told me that he used to call him jokingly 'pareu of Tahiti' because Rupert Brooke could never tie his pareu properly, and it was always falling down! Mauu told me of an old priest who knew the Mamua of the poems, and I went and saw him, and he showed me where Brooke lived at one time, but there was nothing to be seen except jungle growth. He said that Mamua deserved the poems. She was very lovely.

A rat has just run across the floor. I've got used to such things and I don't turn a hair. At the moment I'm sitting on my bed in my yellow and red pareu, and I am thinking that all the world is mad except those of us who live in the South Seas. Your letters, all the letters I'm getting, are chatty and informative but it's amusing to sense the underlying worry and dread that pervade those countries who are the leaders of civilisation. Compare those civilised thoughts with those which exist here. Everyone wants to make love and be happy in undisciplined freedom, and yet mind their own business, and never have an argument . . . on the road if a driver is stupid or a bicyclist is foolish nobody shouts neurotic epithets. Everyone wakes up in the morning seemingly wanting to be happy. Our Western philosophy has become too complicated, losing its way from truth because it is thought clever to do so. Anyhow your letters have made me realise I must stay in the South Seas as long as possible. I'm just off to Taravao two miles from here on my bicycle for a New Year's Eve party. I'm the only European who will be there, and yet I'll not feel an interloper because there is no colour consciousness.

January 1st, 1939.

Happy New Year! I went to Taravao last night and on my way there I was caught in a terrific storm and got very wet. Then when I arrived I had a couple of Aaorai beers and went to a cinema which was in a barn and there were three young men who accompanied the film on their guitars though when the scenes got very exciting they stopped playing. The film was a wildly simple one made at the time, I should imagine, when we were schoolboys in Cologne. It was silent of course and the captions were in English but these were translated into Tahitian by a shrieking man at the back who had a continuous battle against the noise of the rain on the roof and the yells of the audience who loved it all. Afterwards I joined the party of Madame Kett, Tahitian herself with a half Spanish husband, and drank champagne provided by a Chinese. And everybody kissed each other, and then I trundled home the two and a half miles to Papeari. This morning the festivities have continued as Mauu had a native feast for his family and friends and we've been eating raw fish and curried shrimps and shell fish dressed in coconut juice, and wild chicken, and been drinking rum and red wine. I speak only French and Tahitian, and I even think in the language, and again I was the only European. Everyone is so happy without any sense of guilt for feeling so.

D.

Hotel Tahiti,
Papeete.
January 6th.

Darlings,

I am delightfully, deliciously happy. I woke up this morning around seven and went on to my verandah and within fifty yards was the blue of the lagoon and sailing boats that come from distant islands tied up to the wharf. I have finally made up my mind to stay as long as I can. I'll try and catch a boat for New Zealand on February 16th. Meanwhile I'm going on a glorious adventure voyage to Raiatea, Tahaa and Bora Bora, where the film of Tabu was made and White Shadows of the South Seas; and where they say it is all untouched by the vulgarity and beastliness the white man takes everywhere with him. I go first to Tahaa by a two-masted schooner, and she'll be loaded with cattle and smells and queer traders and Chinamen and Tahitians, and though desperately uncomfortable I will always remember the two days with pleasure. Oh the blue that is just beneath me and the blissful stillness. Just near is a schooner from the Austral Islands and another from the Tuamotus. Did I ever tell you of the old English colonel who won

112

an M.C. at Paschendaele and who is now living incongruously at a beautiful spot in Moorea? He gave me a lecture as to why he was there and he ended by saying: 'There will always be rivalry and bitterness and distrust between nations. They have the tortured minds of Bedlam. There is no rest, no peace. I tell you, sir, when I was part of that world I was the same. I myself was confusion. But here, from this place where we are now, I see that world as if it were a glass bowl and inside are the fishes swimming round and round, without end and without meaning.' All this probably sounds rubbish to you.

D.

Toopua.
February 14th.

Darlings,

I have written you a number of letters but there has been no means to take them away from Bora Bora, and so they will go with this one, and you will read about my different moods one after another. But I'll never be the same again after being on this island of Toopua. Only one family living here and it takes an hour to walk round, and it is twenty minutes across the lagoon from Bora Bora There is a hill in the middle and I walked up it this morning and looked across the lagoon to the coral reef guarding the islands from the sea, and to my right was the mountain of Bora Bora and at its base the village of Vaitape edged by the greens and blues of the water, and almost hidden in the coconut trees except for the red brick spire of the church. I could hear a guitar and a man's voice singing.

My hut has a floor of white sand and the sand continues (there is no door) until the water laps it a few yards away and when I lie on my bed I can see the outlines of the coral rocks under the water and the multicoloured fish swimming amongst them, so clear is it. How seldom a dream comes true untarnished, but it has happened to me. And I am so cut off from the world that I really don't mind I now can't catch the boat for New Zealand. Hopelessly irresponsible I know! But the wind has been wrong for the schooner which was

113

coming here, and I may have to wait days. I'm just not thinking what I'll have to do. And yet I am aware in my heart that I don't want to stay for ever among such happiness and that when you are young you must have a purpose to drive you. I just want to cram as many first hand experiences in my life as possible, then sit back and contemplate as to what I've done, thankful that reality has taught me and not second-hand stories. One day perhaps I will find an environment as peaceful and happy as my island of Toopua, and for the rest of my life I will be searching for it.

D.

ss *Stella Polaris*.
February 18th.

Dear all of you,

The doubts and fears and the old restlessness of mind are back. Here I am in the *Stella Polaris* along with a cargo of American millionaires and young heiresses. They sailed into Bora Bora on a world cruise yesterday morning, and I had to make up my mind immediately whether to sail in her or stay here indefinitely. We're now on our way to Pago Pago where Maugham wrote *Rain*, then Samoa, then Suva where I get off and take a boat to New Zealand. So the programme is on again, and I'm absolutely determined to come home via the Trans-Siberian if war has not already broken out. It is the only thing I can do to compensate me leaving my island of Toopua.

Meanwhile half the passengers disapprove of my presence, the other half are curious. I wear only a pareu and am bare-footed. I have one small suitcase because the rest I left behind in Papeete and I've wired the consul to send it on; and I'm quite sure the Captain is also doubtful about me. I've had to explain to him that I can't pay the fare till I arrive at Suva.

As for myself, I find that all my peace of mind has gone.

D.

TEN

I completed the journey as I had planned. A brief sojourn in Auckland with my uncle; a happy time in Sydney and Melbourne, stops at Brisbane and Thursday Island, through the Torres Strait and the Arafura Sea in a Japanese ship to Manila and Hong Kong. A week of Shanghai night life, then Tokyo and a wait for my Soviet visa before setting off for Korea and Manchuria on board the Trans-Siberian Express at Harbin. Ten days on the train silently sharing my compartment with two soldiers, an old woman and a little girl who every night periodically woke up crying in a small agonised voice: 'Mama! Mama!' Moscow, Warsaw, Berlin, and a sight of Hitler shouting. Cologne, and a visit to the Bismarck statue around which I used to play as a child, a day in Paris, then emotionally seeing the white cliffs of Dover. In early June my journey was over.

I went down to Cornwall with my mother and father, then once again I was living in 20 Elm Park Lane. I was in a vacuum. Articles I had written while away had not been published, articles I now proposed were turned down before I wrote the first paragraph. Hitler dominated insular Britain, and yawns greeted my suggestions of stories in other parts of the world. There was no interest in Australia or New Zealand, no interest, in fact, in any part of the British Empire as it was then called. Its loyalty was taken for granted, and no one asked me when I got back how these people, thousands of miles away, would react. There was an unthinking self confidence they would come and help us if need be; and they did.

Yet I found only the few accepted war as inevitable. Hitler

115

of course, provided the main source of conversation but only in the sense that his behaviour was like that of an annoying wasp; and the newspapers gave the impression that they headlined his pronouncements because they were a free gift to the circulation departments during the summer season. Nobody wanted to think, and perhaps they were right; news of the Nazi-Soviet Pact was to come soon enough. I went down to the Isle of Wight for the week-end to stay at the house that the mothers of my friends Bill and Lindsay Baxter and Ward Thompson had rented. Val Hussey was there, and James Mason languidly helping us all relax. During that week-end we revelled in the irresponsible gaiety of optimism; and within two years only James and I were alive, except for the mothers.

I had no wish to find a job because if I did I would not be able to write the book about my travels, and it was this book which held my future, or so I thought. But if I had no job I could not afford to live in London. Hitler would not attack until the harvest was gathered in ... was a current, comforting belief; and so I reckoned I had two months, and I asked 'Beakers' Penrose in Cornwall if he knew of a cottage where I could be alone for that time. He always helped his friends, and soon he found me Rose Cottage.

Rose Cottage was in a wood above Coombe near Truro, and I visited it not long ago with Jeannie. The roof had caved in and brambles thickly covered the path leading to the door; and although the two rooms on the ground floor were clear in their shape to me, I had difficulty in outlining them to Jeannie. They had lost their shape except in my memory. Here Roy, successor to my first old English sheep dog Lance, shared my days and nights, as I toiled at my book. Off we went together on walks during that heavenly summer, and he lay at my feet as I tapped at my typewriter. At the beginning of August I had at last struggled to

116

complete two chapters and I sent them to a friend for approbation. His reply made me tear them up.

A passer-by told me that Ribbentrop had signed the Nazi-Soviet Pact with Molotov; and I remembered the American journalist in Moscow who had said to me, in regard to Britain's own wooing of Stalin, that the Russians thought us utterly insincere because the negotiations were in the hands of William Strang, a Foreign Office official, instead of a Minister. And so I heard the news, and patted Roy on his shaggy head, and said soon he would have to go back to my mother and father.

There is a telephone box above the creek at Coombe, and that evening I rang my brother Nigel. He said that he himself, a Reserve Flying Officer in the RAF, was probably being appointed to Training Command; and that Colin, because of his knowledge of German, had been asked to join the German section of Intelligence. I left the stuffy telephone box knowing that the moment of truth had arrived for me, and that I had to make up my mind what to do. I no longer could try to be myself. I had to conform.

I enlisted in the Duke of Cornwall's Light Infantry a couple of days afterwards and my Company was despatched to Pendennis Castle at Falmouth where our task was to guard the docks. We had no training and we had no weapons except for one rifle which was assigned to a coloured boy to prove there was no colour prejudice in the Army. I alertly patrolled the dock with a stick, and soon realised to my surprise that the opportunity existed for me to continue writing my book. My father had given me a £25 car, and when I discovered that no one objected to me parking it in the dockyard, it became my office; and in between patrolling the quays, during my rest periods, I used to sit in the front seat typing my experiences of the year before.

117

I had written five chapters when news of my scamper through Asia reached the War Office, and I was summoned to London. The brigadier who interviewed me seemed immensely impressed that I had volunteered, and he stared at my crumpled battledress murmuring: 'Damned fine show, damned fine show.' There was, of course, at this time no urgency in the fight against Hitler; and there was even a general air of contentment that the war, without bringing danger, had introduced a spark of purpose into dull lives. We all could feel important without too much concern. Thus I was scarcely surprised when the brigadier informed me that I was the man the country needed to look after the Order of Battle of the Chinese armies, nor when I was quickly made an officer, nor when a week later I was promoted Captain; for such an undeserved meteoric rise from the ranks was not unusual at the time. I had a few days leave in Cornwall, then drove up to London with my mother, and as we passed through Andover I saw an evening paper placard: '*Royal Oak* sunk in Scapa Flow.' I groaned, but my mother beside me said cheerfully: 'You'll have to get used to news like that, dear. We had to last time before we won.'

I sat in my room in the War Office, and found I was not only in charge of the Chinese Order of Battle. I had under my command the British interpretation of the activities of the Netherland East Indies Army, the Thai Army, and that of Indo-China. I had a card index for each army, the names of the officers and sketches of their careers, and I had maps with little flags denoting divisions which I moved about after finding informative paragraphs in *The Times*; for most of the information upon which I based my assessment, eventually if need be the Government's assessment, came from published paragraphs in *The Times*.

My Far East interests did not prevent me from observing what went on elsewhere. Indeed had I known what fascinating secrets I was to harbour during the next few years, and had I been a General, I would have kept a diary of them. I had, however, a sense of responsibility which made me worry that I might lose such a diary or someone unfriendly to the cause might pinch it. But sometimes I was so enraged by what I saw and heard that I allowed myself to scribble mysterious notes which years later I found difficulty in deciphering, so obscure had I made their meaning.

I was the War Office night duty officer when the Germans invaded Norway, the link between the outside military world and the Chiefs of Staff. I was resting on my iron bedstead when the telephone rang and a reporter from the *Daily Express* asked: 'Does the War Office know the Germans are in Norway?' I replied: 'No, thanks for the tip.'

Thereupon I contacted a senior officer in bed at home.

'Hitler's invaded Norway, sir.'

A pause.

'What a bloody fool the man is. Act quickly and we've got him.'

I found such obstinate, unreasonable confidence, time and again; and as an amateur I was bewildered. These military men of power were entrenched by pre-conceived ideas, and if anyone dared doubt them the reply was a stony stare or a bad tempered shout of: 'Nonsense!'

I remember the harassed senior officer garnering information for the statement to be made by Neville Chamberlain to the House of Commons about Norway. He glared at a meek junior officer who had told him Narvik had been captured. 'Dammit,' he said, 'you've got the letter wrong. It can't be Narvik, it must be Larvik.' Narvik was in the north, Larvik in the south; and of course Narvik had been taken by surprise.

And as our ill-equipped troops were about to land in Norway, urgent requests were made as to the conditions they might find. For instance: 'Is the railway line, Stoeren to Lillehamer, narrow or broad gauge?' Answer from the Norwegian Intelligence Section: 'Don't know.'

I kept wondering what these Intelligence Sections had been doing in peacetime and realised that their members, bereft of imagination, found life more rewarding spending their time writing and reading meaningless minutes. But the Norwegian campaign nudged the Chiefs of Staff to look into the matter and General Ismay on their behalf circulated a gentlemanly directive. 'I think,' he wrote, 'we were badly let down over the Norway affair and I think country sections should start immediately to collect proper data . . .'

I happened to be night duty officer again when the invasion proper began, and this time I heard the news over a crackling line from the Military Attaché in Brussels. Once again I forthwith contacted a senior officer. 'The balloon is up, sir,' I said. Came the reply: 'Good . . . now we can get moving.'

I continued, during the days which followed, to play with my divisions of the Chinese Order of Battle. All of us kept stiff upper lips, continued to write unnecessary minutes, and made silly little jokes to hide our increasing anxiety. We pounced on the top secret telegrams which were passing round the sections, and when the Dunkirk evacuation began we hastened in the morning to see the night duty officer who gave us the latest tally of the troops who had got away. I wrote a memorandum to a certain VIP proposing every man and woman should be mobilised into a defence force, and that an intelligence network (local agents, radio communications, etc.) should be formed immediately in those areas likely to be invaded. 'I always like new ideas,' was the reply, 'and for that reason your letter of May 20th was welcome. I do not say that what you suggest is practical, but it will receive consideration when plans are evolved.' It was obvious that there was not a minute to be wasted, and I talked to Michael Foot who at that time was writing superb leaders for the *Evening Standard*. He wrote a clarion call for civilian mobilisation and said he would talk to Beaverbrook. But it was a while later before Anthony Eden announced the formation of the LDV, later the Home Guard.

France fell, and we were advised to carry revolvers; but there were no revolvers. Then my brother Colin who worked in a room along the corridor from me remembered the two Mausers my father had in a show case at Glendorgal; and my father sent them to us along with some ancient looking bullets. One Saturday the two of us had a good lunch and went out to Richmond Park. We were wary of the safety of the Mausers which had been collected from dead Germans in the First World War by my father. So we loaded one of them, tied it to a tree with it pointing to another tree, attached a long piece of string to the trigger, then burst out laughing . . . and pulled. A shot cracked. The Mauser did not explode.

I had finished my travel book by the time the uselessness of my job had been realised and I had been sent on a Course to Swanage. I showed the manuscript to Alec Waugh who was on the Course too, and he liked it mainly because he had been in Tahiti too; and while the Battle of Britain was fought over our heads, and after each day of being taught World War One methods of warfare, we reminisced. 'When the war is over,' he said optimistically, 'you and I will go to Tahiti together.'

I had no faith in myself as an army officer serving in unit, and the Course was leading me that way. I did not seem to grasp the details which were essential if I were to be efficient. I was as dumb as when I used to fail at my examinations at Harrow. I also rejected blind obedience. I just could not see the point of risking my life carrying out some plan which I knew was idiotic. Hence, when towards the end of the Course I was summoned to London, to Wormwood Scrubbs, temporary headquarters of MI5, interviewed by a chain-smoking lady in a ground floor cell and told ten minutes later I had been appointed to MI5, I felt thankful I was to remain an individual. I was to be a member of MI5 in war and in peace for the next ten years.

I was sent first to Newcastle where I worked as an assistant to a delightful man who exasperated me. He was an old hand in MI5 and as a novice I was clearly in no position to query his views. I found, however, that whenever I suggested a possible line of investigation, his logical arguments against pursuing such an investigation speedily deflated me. We were poles apart in our thinking. My experience as a newspaper man had taught me that hunches could lead to a big story, and I believed the same kind of hunches might lead to catching spies. Hunches first, then painstaking investigation. But my boss did not believe in such things, and in this he was like many people I have known in my life. I have been vexed so often by those who go only by the book. Those with grooved minds who obstinately refuse to be flexible.

I had been a month in Newcastle with little to do when I was ordered back to London and instructed to form a special unit where my journalistic experiences could be of value. I was given a cell in Wormwood Scrubbs, a pretty secretary, and freedom to move around the various departments asking what questions I liked to ask . . . for part of my new job was to produce a weekly news-sheet containing the activities of each department. I soon realised that in some quarters I was viewed with suspicion. Wasn't the fellow on the *Daily Express*? Even the *Mirror*? I was surrounded by a plethora of solicitors, barristers, dons, all of whom had arrived to augment the tiny permanent peacetime group of MI5, and I realised I was the odd man out. I had, however the usual ace up my sleeve ... I could not be quite as bad a risk as I appeared to be because my father had been an Intelligence Officer AND I had been at Harrow. Public schoolboys, in those days, could not be traitors. I was tolerated therefore. I was a member of the caste. The truth is that when I joined MI5, it was being geared to combat the Germans; and the Germans as an Intelligence force had the rating of a Fourth Division football team. MI5, except in one, small, ignored corner of the organisation, was bewildered when faced by the naughty deceit of the Russians. Burgess, Maclean and Philby were already in orbit ... but they could act with gay confidence. They knew their caste.

I had not been long in Wormwood Scrubbs before it was decided to evacuate MI5 to the country. The bombs were falling on London and one of them could have destroyed the MI5 records; and so a place was chosen for us to move to, and the place was Blenheim Palace where the Duke of Marlborough and his family surrendered huge rooms to trestle tables.

I realised now that the time had come for me to leave 20 Elm Park Lane, and that when I did so I would in effect be saying goodbye to my youth. There I lived the gay days when there were oceans of time in which to make mistakes and to recover from them; and to be in despair at one moment but be filled with hope the next because there were so many years ahead. I lived there the time which one never expects to end, the ebullience of being young and successful, of passing fancies, of dominating views, of believing all youth is Peter Pan. I gave in my notice to the landlord, then although this notice had a period in which to expire, I decided to take away from the threat of bombs those possessions of mine which I valued most. There was a small kneehole desk of rosewood; my personal papers; a watercolour by Adrian Daintrey; and above all a small oil painting of a plantation

123

and a lagoon by a strange man called Gouwe with whom I had stayed on the island of Raiatea near Tahiti. These were my treasures.

I piled them into my car and drove them to Blenheim Palace, and I carried them into the room which had been chosen for me as my office. It was on the first floor of the south wing, above the archway which all of us used to reach the quadrangle. There they were, safe from the bombs, daily reminding me of normal times.

I was billeted a couple of miles away and in the morning I drove to Blenheim Palace. And one day as I neared the Palace, I saw a plume of smoke curling from the rooftops; and as I drove nearer still, I saw it was coming from a room above the archway. A crowd was standing there, a fire engine was hosing, when I pulled up. And there was also my pretty secretary.

'*Our* room,' she said, looking upwards.

Smoke was now billowing from the window.

A cleaner had inadvertently dropped a match in the wastepaper basket, and set the room ablaze.

ELEVEN

In the New Year I had begun to spend two nights a week at the Savoy, and my book *Time Was Mine* was published, and I met Jeannie; after the second occasion of having dinner with her, a bomb hit the hotel killing two guests, while I was asleep in the shelter knowing nothing about it. The Savoy was the headquarters of the American journalists, indeed of all top journalists, and it was useful for me to be with them. They all hovered round Jeannie who was barely out of her teens, and who was just beginning her reign as the most famous public relations officer the Savoy has ever had. She introduced them to the people they wanted to meet, booked their rooms, flirted with them, and was all the while in a gentle fashion seeing they were happy in London; and in so doing she was able often to influence their reports on Britain.

I was treated as a casual admirer but the people she wanted to know were also the people I wanted to know; and if we were not together we were frequently in the same party. We would be in Tich's Bar for instance. Tich was a bouncy little waiter of much character, and his Bar was not really a Bar but a collection of small tables and chairs on a landing, one floor up from the Embankment entrance. Here, into the early hours of the morning while the guns boomed outside, would come the men who moulded world opinion, the war correspondents and the political commentators; and they would sit, glasses repeatedly re-filled by Tich, arguing over the conduct of the war, recounting rumours, theoretically reshuffling the Cabinet, attacking the censor, discussing individual politicians and generals, revealing the trends of

Britain and of America and elsewhere. Jeannie was often with them and although she was very feminine I noticed they treated her as one of their own; and I remember her at a corner table with Quentin Reynolds, helping him prepare one of his famous broadcasts.

Within a day or two of *Time Was Mine* being published, the whole stock was destroyed when a bomb landed on the warehouse in which the copies were housed; and a week or two later the printing works was hit. No books and no type, and the publishers refused to reprint; and so it was a quick end to the high hopes I once had of my round the world story. Yet a few copies circulated and I had some rewards . . . the legendary Hannen Swaffer who had always seemed a god to me wrote a page about it, then I met him, and he said in his slow cockney voice, a stub of a cigarette in the corner of his mouth, ash over his lapels, wispy untidy white hair, a high collar and a black cravat: 'I don't read books . . . I've read yours . . . damned good.' High praise indeed from Swaff; and he was always to be my friend, and Jeannie's to whom he inscribed a photograph he gave her when we left for Cornwall: 'To Jean, in disgust with her for running away.' And there were humorous rewards too. A colleague in M15 said to me pompously on the steps of Blenheim Palace: 'You'll regret this book, Tangye, when you're older.' And shortly after Jeannie and I were married, one old lady who was our neighbour said to another old lady: 'I *do* hope Mrs Tangye hasn't read Mr Tangye's book.' And there was the vicar of St Columb near Newquay who denounced me from the pulpit for my frankness, much to the amusement of his parishioner, my father; for I had dedicated the book to my father and mother.

By May I was beginning to see Jeannie more regularly. I had been shifted back to London and because my work was of a special nature I was given a private flat to use as my office where I could be on my own, away from the formalities of headquarters. There was, however, the question of where to live, and this was solved one day when I met an American lady who had temporarily married into the Peerage. She had a furnished house to let on the river a few hundred yards below Richmond Bridge; and as soon as I saw it I fell in love with it . . . and at Cholmondeley House, nearly two years away, Jeannie and I held our wedding reception.

Of course it was much too large for me on my own, but two American journalists were with me on the day I first saw it, and we agreed to share it together. There was a beautiful room on the first floor with bay windows overlooking the river, and I was to stand there hour after hour observing the dirty old barges with jaunty names like *Pam* and *Willie*, or staring at the passers-by on the towpath during warm evenings and sunny week-ends, uniforms of all defeated nations and those of the Commonwealth; and the girls. There was an island opposite, a deserted island of undergrowth and trees; that first spring swans had a nest there, and I came to the house in time to watch the cygnets have their first swim. Richmond at this period seemed to be a village and I believed I lived in the most beautiful part of it; but as I said Cholmondeley House was too large for me on my own. The dining room was as big as the room on the first floor and there were five bedrooms and two gardens; a tiny one between the house and the towpath, a larger one at the back alongside the garage which you walked through from Friars Lane to reach the front door. Bachelors couldn't run the house on their own and because the organisation was left to me, I chose the housekeeper to look after us. I did not know that one of my partners was never to appear again, the other was seldom to pay. But I had other friends who stayed from time to time as paying guests, and so I managed to

127

continue to live apparently beyond my means; and to pursue the job which enabled me to serve the men of power.

As the months went by it became a habit for people to come out to Cholmondeley House on Sundays, and from lunchtime to late in the evening there would be talk; and it became a kind of extension of Tich's Bar without the drink. Any subject might be discussed, any political argument debated. It was an uncomfortable period of doubts and suspicions, of views too vehemently expressed as a result; and the views might lunge in one direction one Sunday, the opposite direction the next. Cholmondeley House was a turbulent barometer.

Was Lloyd George, for instance, preparing himself to be the British Petain? The picture of the man suited the conjectures; his magic, a contemporary of Petain in age and war experience, the memory of his years of glory leading him to yearn for power again whatever the conditions might be. He fed the rumours around his name by giving occasional injudicious interviews to American editors on fleeting tours of Britain. One or two of these editors, ostensibly on a mission of top level reporting, were also emissaries of the Administration. America was still not in the war, and the scouts were searching for frailties in our determination.

I do not think the British took the stories about him seriously because we were all so conceited that we could not believe it possible a British Petain would be needed. The Americans were different. They watched from afar and many doubted our stamina; and so when Lloyd George unburdened his fears in 'off the record' interviews, there were some who believed him. I remember one American who arrived during 1941 with a letter of introduction to Churchill from President Roosevelt who went post haste to see Lloyd George at Churt; and when afterwards I saw him he said: 'The old man was terribly depressed. He believes he is the only man who can negotiate a peace in any way favourable to Britain. He is convinced you cannot win the war on your own.' I do not suppose this particular American realised that Lloyd George was only getting rid of a mood when he talked in this way. His indiscretions were not calculated ones; and on great occasions it is the calculated indiscretion which you have to watch for in the political arena. Lloyd George was old, and tired, and sad.

But by June we were no longer alone. The Germans had attacked the Soviet Union, and suddenly Stalin was being cheered instead of being booed when he appeared on the newsreels. In December the Japanese bombed Pearl Harbor, and the Germans declared war on America. 'At last after two years we're in,' said Quentin Reynolds wryly, 'and we've managed it without declaring war on anyone.' And as for ourselves there now began the period of Churchill baiting.

One of my jobs was to keep in regular contact with the Secretary of the War Cabinet, the present Lord Bridges; and though this did not mean I was in possession of high level secrets, I probably knew more from my various sources about government activities than most of the critics to whom I listened; and I may have been right when I thought that Churchill's basic problem was the 'dead wood' he inherited when he took office.

This 'dead wood', those people in key positions of varying degree and placed in so many arms of government, both military and civil, were momentarily galvanised into life when Britain was on her own, but soon slipped back into their mediocre ways when the acute danger was over. These were the same people who muddled the country into war unprepared, the type who were responsible for the Norway fiasco, the same who helped the British Empire to die from boredom. There were tiers of such people and Churchill, absorbed by great decisions, could not get rid of them in a matter of months or a year or two because there were so many of them. They sat snugly in their homes and offices, hindering Britain's future by their lack of imagination. Churchill was aware of this, and it made him depressed and irritable. He was, like most men of brilliance, absurdly affected by the lowering influence of the third rate.

Hence the biting tongue of Aneurin Bevan, Churchill's most publicised critic, was a blessing in disguise. He may have angered Churchill but he was the only person to provide him with a rhetorical opposition in the House of Commons; and thus he also stimulated Churchill. The trouble with Nye Bevan, a man of such charm and wit and explosive oratory, was that he often allowed his emotions to influence his judgement; he made Churchill into a permanent Aunt Sally, Churchill could never do right.

Yet the venom of Nye Bevan was directed at the people who sheltered behind Churchill rather than Churchill himself. He was concerned with the class war as well as the fighting war; and when he lashed Churchill, he was in fact lashing the old order which he considered Churchill represented. But Nye Bevan's weakness lay in his interpretation of the facts upon which he based his talk and speeches. Too often his arguments seemed to fit his wishful thinking; and a speech, hailed as brilliant by his devoted band of admirers, would thus fail to hit the target because the content was too obviously tainted by prejudice.

Jeannie and I dined with him one night soon after the battle of El Alamein in a small restaurant off Leicester Square. A victory at last but Nye would not admit it, and he was wailing as usual about Churchill's conduct of the war. 'What does this victory mean?' he asked. 'If instead we'd sent our forces to Europe and left a holding force at El Alamein, the war would be over now. The opportunity was missed, and we've lost the war, we've lost the war . . .' Then he continued: 'We must find a Prime Minister who will choose Ministers who will purge their departments of all incompetents. Up to now it is the *people* of Britain who have carried Britain through, not the leaders or the ruling class.' And then, as often happened with him, his mood suddenly changed. He began laughing.

'The other night,' he said in his lilting Welsh voice, 'I had dinner with a Colonel in the War Office. The man said the House of Commons should be closed so that the leaders could get on with the war undisturbed. Fancy now, fancy saying a thing like that.' He had turned to Jeannie and was wagging a finger at her. 'So what could I say in the circumstances? "You're a middle class Fascist!" I shouted across the dinner table. The chap was very annoyed.' Nye paused again, the joke was ready. 'And what was he annoyed about? He didn't at all mind being called a Fascist . . . but I ought to have called him upper class!'

He never allowed his political convictions to interfere with his enjoyment of good living. Larry Rue, the pro-British correspondent of the *Chicago Tribune*, used to tease him about this. One day the three of us were having lunch together in the Savoy Grill when Nye complained about the food. He did not think it up to the usual standard. 'Ah,' said Larry mockingly, 'now you know how the poor live.'

Some people at one stage even wanted Sir John Anderson to take over from Churchill, but fortunately the idea petered out. It was during the period between the fall of Singapore and the victory of El Alamein, surely the worst period in Churchill's life, and men around Churchill were becoming exasperated by his refusal to listen to anyone. 'I sometimes think,' said one Minister acidly to me, 'that when Churchill wishes to carry out an important operation he considers the speech he can make about it first . . . then decides how the operation is to be carried out.' Unfair, but the comment represented the mood.

Towards the end of that year of El Alamein I spent a fascinating afternoon with Harold Macmillan. (My reason for interviewing him concerned a book I was writing about the British Empire, of this more later.) It was just before he was appointed Resident Minister in North Africa, and he was at that time Under Secretary for the Colonies. I saw him at the Colonial Office, and for a couple of hours I was alone with him except for occasional darting appearances of John Wyndham his aide, now Lord Egremont. Macmillan was then comparatively unknown, and I knew no one who tipped him as a future Prime Minister, nor was he a politician whose views were much discussed. He was just an efficient Under Secretary, a little frustrated by his job, yet soon to be on his way to take a place in history. There he sat at his desk, a rakish air about him, a sonorous musical voice dropping elegant witticisms, loads of charm, and inquisitive. He was also suffering.

'Wyndham!' he called, after I had been there a short while, and a door opened and Wyndham hurried through it, tall and thin, eager, attentive, like the head boy of a school seeking to please his headmaster. 'Wyndham, I am in great pain . . . bring me a bottle of whisky.' The pain was the legacy from his severe wounds in the First World War. Wyndham fetched the bottle.

'First help Mr Tangye liberally to a glass.'

I sat sipping my whisky feeling that perhaps my presence was useful to him because he was in pain and he did not feel in the mood to concentrate his mind on serious matters. And he flattered me by listening to what I had to say, cross questioning me, then giving me his own views and telling me anecdotes.

'I'll never co-operate in an anti-Churchill movement,' he

said, and he made great emphasis on this, 'but he will have to be careful that he doesn't Asquith himself. He is surrounded by a crowd of inefficients. If something goes wrong again people will be crying for another government, and Beaverbrook will be sent for. Beaver will lay down his own terms .. leaving Churchill as a figurehead, and becoming the power behind the scenes, getting rid of committees and so on.'

Wyndham was again at my elbow. 'Thank you,' I said.

'Aristocrats after the war,' Harold Macmillan was saying, 'may complain that they have lost their money and so on . . . but they've ruled England for a long time. They can go on doing so, go on having their shooting and fishing, but they'll have to change their titles to Commissars.'

American troops were now arriving in Britain in great numbers and although fraternisation up to that time had been surprisingly good, many influential Americans continued to bark their jibes about the British Empire. I told Harold Macmillan about the *Time Magazine* Bureau chief who said the British were robbers, and how I had a slanging match with him, yelling: 'Puerto Rico! Philippines! Hawaii!'

'They know nothing about the British Empire,' said Macmillan, half American, 'and it is an illusion that we make money out of the colonies whatever they say. Indeed the African colonies and the West Indies are a liability but of course we have to remember our own people who have made their homes in those places. They work very hard, you know, for very little.'

At this point he was smiling to himself, and so I guessed I was about to listen to a favourite point of view.

'The Yanks,' he said, and a quiet chuckle had already begun, 'always talk of the Boston tea party as the real reason for the American revolution. I never cease reminding my American friends that this is not so. The real reason, I remind them, was an edict of the Duke of Newcastle in 1776 that read something like this: "In the name of George the Third I order all lands to be returned to the Red Indians!" And of course as soon as the American colonials heard this, the revolt was on!'

The black-out hid Whitehall when I came away from his office; and his parting words to me were that he was there from 9.30 in the morning to 8.30 in the evening, and that I would always be made welcome. 'Come whenever you like,' he said, 'and tell me the news.' I never did see him again.

While I had been at Cholmondeley House I had edited a book called *Went The Day Well*. The title came to me during the time M15 was at Blenheim Palace, when I was billeted at a lovely old house in the village of Coombe where a hawk-eyed old lady made a great effort to pretend that my presence in her home was not a considerable nuisance. One day I was looking through her visitors' book and found these two anonymous lines against an entry of 1917:

> Went the day well? We died and never knew.
> But well or ill, England, we died for you.

I was very moved by these lines, and I thought that they exactly suited the theme of the book. I did, however, substitute 'freedom' for 'England' because the book was not only about Englishmen; and, after all, England and freedom were then synonymous. I explained the book in this way:

This is the story of men and women who bade goodbye to their days of peace to die for gains they will never share. They came from many different lands, spoke many different tongues, yet all of them gave their lives for the same beliefs.

They did not want to die. For dying meant leaving good friends, and happy homes, and clear blue skies, and the salt of the sea, and rounds of golf, and walks across the moors, and drinks at the club and the wind at night, and the scent of log fires. For dying meant they would never know whether or not they had fought in vain.

Yet when the moment of cold decision ended the brightness of their lives their thoughts did not halt them; and they died so their beliefs might live.

Some may call them heroes, but they themselves would not wish to be considered such; because each, according to his fashion, did his duty . . . expecting neither reward nor recognition.

There is, then, no special standard of conduct in their way of life that has made them part of this story; only that their actions mirror what millions have already done and what millions are prepared to do.

They are of the cavalcade of freedom. Labourers and clerks, playboys and housewives, students and old men, typists and nurses; all these and many more who march the road of danger and sacrifice so that the lights of cities may blaze again and the lands be filled with song.

One Friday last November I spent an evening with a young Polish Air Force officer called 'Vladek' Grudzinski. In the passage of time I had not known him long; in the quality of mutual friendship I might have known him since the days he patrolled the skies above Warsaw. He was twenty-four, small like a jockey, with a round face and fair hair, and eyes that from being laughing and kind would at the mention of Nazi Germany suddenly look cold and cruel. He had fought almost continuously for two years and three months – in Poland, France and England. He had just been decorated with the Polish Cross after shooting down his seventh enemy plane in this country.

On that evening he was very happy. The English girl he loved had said she too loved him. For the first time, perhaps, since leaving Poland, he had someone to live for; because he had not heard of his family since the beginning of the war.

There was a cold moon lighting the house-tops of London when I said goodbye to him, and I remember well the shaft of silver light on his face as he leaned out of his car to wave goodnight. 'Till next week ' he laughed

But there was no next week

135

On Sunday morning he was out on a sweep over France with his squadron. Over Dunkirk he dived within fifty feet of an anti-aircraft battery, spraying it with bullets. As he pulled out of the dive a shell from the battery caught his plane amidships and blew it to pieces. Another gay life had gone.

Another gay life to join the procession of those who have died for the rest of us to go on living. Full of hope and courage and love of being alive. Unstinting in their willingness to sacrifice. Sure that the future will dawn bright. Firm in their faith that those who are left will not fail.

And so it was that on that evening when I heard the news of 'Vladek' Grudzinski I thought of the story of this book. A story not to be written by a single person, but by a company of people each of whom had known the savagery of personal loss. A story that would tell how men and women of this age lived full lives and met sudden deaths. How they gloried in doing their duty and how they paved the way for life to become normal again. How courage was their companion and tenacity their sword. How they were strong in defeat and sharp in attack.

Men and women who, through the centuries to come will always be remembered.

This is the story . .

I had asked a number of people, both known and un-known, to write of someone who had been killed during the first two years of the war, and whom they had cared for. Patricia Ward wrote of Billy Fiske, the American who volunteered for the RAF and who was killed in the Battle of Britain, the first American pilot to die in the war; there were tributes to the two MPs Ronald Cartland and Arnold Wilson, the latter a disillusioned appeaser who joined the RAF as soon as he realised he had been wrong, and was killed at the age of fifty-six serving as an air gunner; James Agate, the diarist and theatrical critic, wrote of the gay young Tony Baerlein, and introduced an Agate note on the day the book was published by telling me it had been published at the wrong time; the then Bishop of Southwark wrote of Prebendary Thompson who was killed by a bomb as he stood on the steps of St Peter's, Eaton Square, where he had been vicar for twenty-five years; Peter Quennell wrote of Christopher Hobhouse; Howard Spring wrote his little masterpiece about a conscientious objector, Arnold Baker, who was prepared to die as a merchant seaman but not as a member of the armed forces; there were stories about the MacRobert brothers whose mother bought a bomber as a memorial and presented it to the RAF, about a WVS member, about an auxiliary fireman named Jack Maynard and written by Hannen Swaffer ('Does it stand up to the others?' he had asked), about a housewife, and an ambulance driver, and a member of the Rescue Service; there were the stories of Sergeant Pilot Ward, the New Zealand VC, of other representatives of the Dominions and India; there were tributes to Ludovic Kennedy's father, Captain Coverley Kennedy, captain of the *Rawalpindi*, the armed merchant cruiser with six inch guns which attacked the *Deutschland* and was destroyed; each conquered country had a representative, and the Soviet Union, our then only fighting ally, had a tribute written by Leonide Bondarenko, the Tass Agency man, who was my friend and who often came to Richmond. All these stories had been written by people who, at some moment of a day, had heard the news that a friend had been killed, and felt despair. I ended the book with an epilogue:

... That is the story. If, having read it, we have a feeling of grimness it will not have been told in vain. For if out of the pages there stepped a ghost he might tell us there are some who forget, who forget the dead who died for them, who forget the blind who were blinded for them, who forget the maimed who were maimed for them.

He might ask us to close our eyes sometimes and vision the last moments of some who have gone – the airman who in a spiral dive

137

struggles in vain to free himself from the cockpit; the bomber crew whose plane is ablaze; the seaman who lingers in the icy water; the soldier who chokes on blood in the desert; the patriot who stands against a wall in the dawn with a handkerchief around his eyes.

He might ask us to think sometimes about these men; about the anguish in their hearts and the twisting pain in their bodies; about the loved ones they left behind and about the children they will never see grow old.

He might ask us, then, to swear vengeance; vengeance not only against the enemy, but against the old world which preferred them to die young. He might ask us to show our vengeance, not in our bitterness, but in our defiance of the hell still to come; in our ruthless resolution to win the peace that will come too.

For out of the peace, out of the great new world those who are left will build, these men and women will find their memorial.

No one was paid for their contributions, and all royalties went to the Prisoner of War Section of the Red Cross; recently the book has been published again and this time the royalties are going to the Star and Garter Home of Rich-mond. During the war each story was broadcast to Occupied Europe and messages were received by the BBC asking for them to be repeated. My generation does not forget these men and women and what they did for us; but there are the others, who take the present for granted.

There was for me a sequel to *Went The Day Well*. A few days after it was published I was standing one Sunday afternoon with Jeannie at one of the windows of that lovely room of Cholmondeley House overlooking the river, when we saw below us on the towpath a legless member of the Star and Garter Home cruising slowly along in his wheel-chair; and on his machine was tied a Union Jack. We both felt the same. *There* was a man who had lost all the normal pleasures of living by serving the ideals of his country, and still had the faith he had done right. Of course, now in retrospect, I realise that we were being sentimental, but we both felt at the time enriched that there were people who believed that the British had something to be proud of. The man still had not wheeled his way out of sight when I excitedly turned to Jeannie.

'I've got it ... I'm going to write a book as to why that man still has faith!'

She looked at me, not knowing me except for the times we had been gaily together, a little suspicious of my sudden enthusiasm, ready to please but feeling she should be sensible.

'What sort of book?'

'I'll try and explain why he feels as he does.'

'You can't just write about enthusiasm.'

'There'll be more to it than that.'

I had already slowed down in my excitement; Jeannie, this passing friend beside me, or so she seemed at the time, had brought sense to me. The man in the wheelchair may have given me an idea, but Jeannie had halted me; and as a result during the following few days I looked at the idea pretty coldly, and the next time I saw Jeannie I thanked her for what she had said to me, and I told her she was quite right, and that instead of being emotional, I was going to write a factual account of the British Empire. So factual that my first chapter would be a series of questions: What is a Dominion? What is a Crown Colony? What is a Protectorate? What is a Mandated Territory? What are the powers of a Governor? What is the Executive Council? What is the Legislative Council? I would then write a chapter on every Colony and each Dominion, describing the history, the political and economic situation, and the prospect for the future; and at all times I would try to be objective and let the facts speak for themselves. Of course I had no idea what I had let myself in for; and nor had Jeannie any idea of the part she was going to play. It was going to take two years of my spare time to collect the material and write the book, interviewing scores of people and reading mountains of documents. I was a bachelor when I began it, and a married man of nearly two years when it was published. I had called it *One King*; and the two of us waited anxiously for reaction.

Meanwhile Jeannie began to visit Cholmondeley House regularly on Sundays from her home at St Albans, and I used to walk up Friars Lane to meet her. If I was late I would see her hurrying along under the trees which bordered the Green, and greeting her would tell her who had turned up for the day. Capa always came when he was in London, the legendary Capa who was the greatest war photographer of his generation, and who was killed stepping on a mine in Indo-China; dark and very gentle, with a cigarette drooping out of the corner of his mouth, making one think that he looked like an *apache*. 'Jeannie with the light brown hair,' his soft Hungarian accent would say, 'I love Jeannie with the light brown hair.' This always was his welcome to her. Claud Cockburn who wrote in the *Daily Worker* under the name of Frank Pitcairn, and wrote also a famous newsletter, would regularly display his exuberance; politics for him had the excitement of the countdown before a moonshot ... provided the countdown had hitches. Alec Waugh and Michael Arlen would drift in. Michael Arlen suffered severely from hangovers and usually wore dark glasses, and he was quite unlike the brittle characters he wrote about. He had an immense love, although born an Armenian, for Britain, and he had come back from America and offered to take any job in the Ministry of Information. They gave him a liaison job in their Midland division, and he was content to accept it, and did very well ... until a witch hunt began, and solid British citizens objected to an Armenian speaking for them. 'I had a dirty deal, I know,' he murmured to me one day, 'but who am I to make a fuss? There is a war on and I'm not going to bother the public about my small troubles.'

There were Ned Russell, Bill White and Geoffrey Parsons of the *New York Herald Tribune*, and Cy Sultzberger of the *New York Times*; all of whom believed in the British way of life and never failed to make this clear in their despatches. Arthur Koestler came once or twice, bringing his sadness with him. Shelagh Graham giggled her way through a couple of visits during a trip from America; very feminine, watching all the time for stories with bite for her column, and described by Alec Waugh as a 'dream'. And years later to become famous for her book describing her life with Scott Fitzgerald. Robert St John, the bearded correspondent of the National Broadcasting Corporation, who wrote *From The Land Of Silent People*; and who, when my book *A Gull On The Roof* was published, remembered the times he had had with us at Cholmondeley House, and arranged with a Florentine bookbinder for a copy to be specially bound. And there were the exiles ... Joseph Luns now Foreign Minister of the Netherlands, Milan Gavrilovic the Yugoslav who gave me the wooden pipe bowl I have in front of me at this moment, Poles, Chinese, Norwegians. Jeannie never knew who might be there when she arrived at Cholmondeley House; and quietly took over the role of hostess.

Then at last she became the resident hostess.

'Will you marry me?' It was seven o'clock in the Coalhole the pub in the Strand, and I had been waiting for her for an hour; and she had expected a row as she came up to the marble topped table where I was sitting.

'Yes,' she said quickly, glad to be let off.

TWELVE

We were married in the Lady's Chapel of Richmond Parish Church at quarter past twelve on February 20th. The Russians were destroying the German Army at Stalingrad, the Eighth Army had reached Tunisia; and the little blitz, the flying bombs and the rockets still lay ahead.

We had presented ourselves to the Vicar of Richmond three weeks beforehand, and after agreeing to marry us he asked me to pay his fee. I pulled out my cheque book and started to write. 'I don't accept cheques,' the Vicar said smartly. And as I had no cash, Jeannie had to look in her purse and produce the money; and she says I never paid her back. My mother came up from Cornwall to stay at Cholmondeley House a fortnight before the wedding, reluctantly because she was anxious not to interfere; and then, as soon as she arrived, she caught a bad cold but she wouldn't admit it because all she worried about was being a nuisance. She wasn't, and she helped us both in a thousand quiet ways, and, Jeannie, whom she loved, effortlessly made her realise she was needed.

My brother Colin was best man and as Jeannie came into the church, the organist playing Jerusalem, he murmured to me: 'Give her a winning smile!' She was wearing the veil of the Earl of Dudley's family which had been lent her by Patricia Ward who had written the tribute to Billy Fiske in *Went The Day Well*; and I remember thinking as she looked at me across the church how sweet was a quiff of her dark hair that appeared incongruously out of it. She didn't mean it to be there. She had dressed at the Savoy, surrounded by well-meaning relations who had fussed over her and who had a glorious time pulling the veil this way and that; and the quiff was a result

There was the usual rumbustious reception, and savour was added to the occasion by the Thames threatening to flood the house. It had succeeded often enough before. I would watch it edging across the towpath, into the small garden, up to the French window where a board was supposed to keep it out . . . and then somebody would shout the alarm and I would realise I had been surprised in the rear. For the river would move along Friars Lane and enter the house via the garage, the large garden and the front door. The housekeeper naturally moaned despair, but I, watching from half way upstairs, would have the excitement of a schoolboy. 'Look! It's half way up the legs of the dining table!' or 'It's gone higher than last time!'

Jeannie and I left for our honeymoon as the tide had reached its height, and this time no damage was done, and the guests were safe; all we had to do was to walk nimbly along a small stone wall to the car, wheels awash, which was taking us to Victoria station. We spent our honeymoon at Brighton, and we were both in a daze after the parties which had led up to the wedding; and neither of us remembers very much except buying a Wedgwood jug from a shop in The Lanes which we still have, and spending lunch times at Pitt's Hotel where old man Pitt had lived since 1886; and where a luscious old gentleman named Bimbo, a retired clown, ceremoniously presented Jeannie with his buttonhole each day . . . an orchid, a camellia, and a red rose.

We returned to Cholmondeley House, and were soon informed that as the owner needed it again we had to leave. It was a disappointing beginning to our married life, but we soon had compensation in the excitement of looking for another house; and the house had to be on the river because both of us found peace watching the river. It was a necessary antidote to the life we led. Indeed it became an obsession to find such a house, and when, after weeks of searching, we found one called Mall Cottage in Chiswick Mall whose small garden had a parapet which fell sheer to the river, we were of course delighted. We arranged terms with the owner, and were ready to move in when we had a telegram. The owner had changed his mind. Naturally we were furious, and we did all those things that fury generates . . . consulted solicitors, wrote harsh letters and so on. The owner was unmoved, and so in the end we had to accept defeat. There was, however, an aftermath . . . a year later Mall Cottage had a direct hit, and the bomb went through the sitting-room.

So we were back to the beginning, and time was getting short; and it was then that one Saturday morning I stopped the car on Chiswick Bridge, where we got out, and stared down at the little cluster of houses which huddled along the river in the shadow of the huge Watney brewery building. There were only six, in fact, and a pub . . . Riverside House with its roof blown off, Leyden House where, we were to learn, an indomitable lady crippled by arthritis was looked after by her husband, Thames Bank House where a very old couple also had faced the blitz on their own, Tudor Cottage where dogs barked, Asplin Cottage and Thames Bank Cottage. The little group looked scruffy, no hint of elegance like the houses lining the river at Strand-on-the-Green a couple of miles up river, or those at Chiswick Mall a couple of miles down river. Old cottages and old houses but they were dwarfed by the brewery and I felt that, except for Boat Race day, they represented a forgotten part of the river. Passers-by, I suspected, would look at the brewery not at them.

'I like it down there,' said Jeannie.

'Me too.'

And in five minutes we were in the pub meeting Gus and

Olivette Foster and asking why the cottage, next door to the pub except for a patch of waste land and an elm, was empty. 'The owners, Mr and Mrs Moore, are very particular,' said Mrs Foster primly, eyeing us.

We were to know Mr and Mrs Foster very well. It was easy to call Mr Foster, Gus, while it was impossible to call Mrs Foster, Olivette. They had been at The Ship for thirty years, from the period when maharajahs hired the pub on Boat Race days to the time we came to Mortlake and there was excitement if two customers called during the morning. Gus came from an old Music Hall family ('My father was manager for Lord George Sanger and booked Marie Lloyd for Margate'), and he had met Olivette when she was sixteen and champion diver of London. He had a rakish air, was owner at one time of twenty three trotting ponies one of which, Polly Pan, was the champion of England; and before the First World War he was a member of the National Sporting Club where he puffed cigars, and drank champagne, as he watched the now legendary boxers. Gus was a character, and when later Jeannie and he used to go racing, he always gave her an expensive bunch of flowers. We had many parties at The Ship. We had many occasions singing into the early hours around a battered old piano to the accompaniment of an unreliable Gus; and dear Mrs Foster, enjoying it all immensely herself, used to murmur again and again to herself: 'He's had enough . . . he's had enough.'

The Moores, owners of Thames Bank Cottage, accepted us after careful inspection. The care, as I was to learn, was due to the close knit grouping of the inhabitants of Thames Bank, Mortlake. They wanted the *right* people to live there and be one of themselves, and the *right* people had to belong to their way of thinking. In this, I am afraid, Jeannie and I were a disappointment. We were rather demure when we applied for Thames Bank Cottage. We played down that side of ourselves which steady people might have viewed with alarm; and as a result one glorious day we were told that Thames Bank Cottage was ours to rent at £90 unfurnished a year. I said to Jeannie that we had found the home which would be ours for always.

The cottage had a dunce's cap. The roof, instead of being a normal roof, rose from its four corners to a peak just like those paper hats in a Christmas cracker. The living-room was at the top of the house, oak beamed, and with windows looking across the river to the meadows on the other side, the winning post of the Boat Race almost opposite. On the left was Chiswick Bridge, on the right in the distance the silhouette of London. There was a bathroom on the same floor and in winter it was bitterly cold, and in those days there was no clever way of heating, and so every winter at some time or other the pipes were frozen. The stairs were of polished wood, and on the first floor were the large bedroom also facing the river and a spare bedroom at the back. On the ground floor was the dining-room where Monty of *A Cat In The Window* used to sit watching the passers-by and waiting for us at night to come back. There was the kitchen and off the kitchen was another little bedroom with its own bathroom; and the night before our last Boat Race party Gertrude Lawrence stayed there after her performance in *September Tide*. The small garden had high walls surrounding it, and at the far end was a pillbox of an air raid shelter where we used to crouch with Monty when the little blitz began, except on the night the cottage was full of people celebrating our first wedding anniversary, and the roof was blown off. Jeannie didn't like being in the shelter because she was frightened of the spiders, and she was concerned for the chickens we kept in the chicken house alongside. We grew vegetables in the garden, and planted a syringa bush which became large enough for Monty to shelter under on hot summer days and a cherry tree which he used as a scratching post.

We were lucky in the uneasy married life we led. We were together. We did not have to write letters which might not reach their destination, or wait for letters, or telegrams, or read about faraway news in which one of us might personally be involved. Our unease lay only in the pace of our life, and in the disquiet that we might not be doing enough. We were at the heart of affairs and we had power, and we could often succeed in doing something through our contacts when conventional methods of communication had failed. I always knew, for instance, that any matter raised by me and considered of paramount importance, could be on the Prime Minister's desk within a few hours. Such matters, however, were rare. And sometimes I doubted the worth of my luck, and wondered whether I should apply for a change.

I was still collecting material and writing *One King . . .* fifty thousand words, one hundred thousand words, one hundred and fifty thousand words. I thought the task would never end, and I had to find time at all hours for interviewing people. At night Jeannie would bring me cups of black coffee, and I felt despair at one moment and elation the next when another section of the Empire had been dealt with. I was a joke among my friends, and a nuisance; for when in the evening they were relaxing, I would drag Jeannie away and take her home where she would cook me dinner on the gas stove, and Monty would purr round my legs, and I would force myself to sit at my desk.

Occasionally we would have staying with us a man or a woman who had been on a secret mission to Europe, or someone who had defected to the British. These brave lonely people had an approach to life which shook me into realising that I had nothing in common with them except remote sympathy. I was in the same category as the

Americans who have never known bombs falling on their homeland. Pour out the words of commiseration, the words of admiration, the words of encouragement, but in doing so no hearts are touched except in the imagination.

There was a Pole, thin like a taut wire, who acted as a courier for the Polish underground, and who was perhaps the most important courier of them all. He had been three times out of German occupied Poland, three times back, and he had now brought with him a message from the head of the Jewish secret Socialist party in Warsaw ... a message about the slaughter of Polish Jews in the concentration camps which we in the West refused to believe really existed. In the upstairs room of Thames Bank Cottage, a log fire burning, curtains drawn for the blackout, Jeannie handing round the coffee cups, he described to me the assignment he had been given. He spoke calmly without heroics, and yet I had a strange sense that he knew that the hardest part of his assignment was in the present. He had to convince people like me that he was *speaking the truth*.

He had been ordered, so that the message he brought might be more convincing, to see for himself what happened in a concentration camp. And he told me how he had smuggled himself into a camp with false papers describing him as a German Camp Inspector. He saw an elderly man, naked, emaciated, sitting by himself. No one took any notice. He saw a dead baby on the floor. Nobody took any notice.

He described to me how there was a wooden passage leading to a railway. Thirty wagons were entrained there, each wagon had room for forty people. At a signal the Gestapo guards started shouting, and the Polish Jews in a panic rushed down the wooden passage and into the wagons. Instead of forty in each wagon, there were at least a hundred, and all the while the guards were shooting and punching and beating with sticks; and then drove more into each wagon, forcing them to climb over the dying bodies of the others. 'The train shuddered with their cries,' said the Pole. Then the doors were banged shut, and the mass in each wagon continued to scream; and the guards laughed because they knew what soon was to happen. The floor of each wagon had been covered with lime, and fumes began to fill each one; and no person survived.

There is no answer to such a story which, at that period of time, was one among many competing for newspaper head-lines. No answer at all except the inward knowledge that one had been hearing the ring of truth; and that politicians should hear about it and everybody else who had time to listen. But the Pole already had the answer to my thoughts.

'When I left,' he said, 'when I left Warsaw my chief who has lived in the West said to me: "They will not believe you, Witold. They will listen politely but they will not understand . . . you will be pleased because you have been invited to see an important person, and you will arrive at his office at half past eleven in the morning. You will give him all the evidence, you will be getting eloquent, you will be saying what we want done . . . then at quarter to one your listeners will look at their watches and one of them, to the delight of the others, will say it is lunchtime, and the interview will be over. They will not understand, Witold." '

The Polish link in London of the Socialist underground in Warsaw was called Sieglebaum. The Pole who was sitting in our upstairs room delivered to him the message which he had been ordered to give. 'You must tell the British and the Americans that they *must* make reprisals if any Jew in Poland is to survive. I beseech you!'

Shortly after receiving the message Sieglebaum committed suicide. 'I have failed,' he wrote in a letter he left, 'but perhaps by the way of my death, the world may be told what I was not able to tell in my life.'

He failed again Only the few believed what was happening. The others waited for the evidence of their eyes.

Periodically, A. P. Herbert, on river patrol, would moor the *Water Gypsy* opposite us, and row ashore in peak cap and Petty Officer's uniform. Sometimes it was in the morning before we were up when we would hear the bleep bleep of the hooter announcing his arrival; sometimes it was late at night. I suppose the most satisfactory period of his life was when he, as a Petty Officer and a Member of Parliament, patrolled the Thames in his beloved *Water Gypsy*.

'Did you know,' he said as we had breakfast on a sunny September morning, sitting on the steps of the cottage during one of his early calls, 'that over there, under the towpath by the brewery, were buried hundreds of victims of the Plague?' And he went on about the cottage. 'It may have been the original inn because the legend is that it was kept by a waterman who married a Shakespeare player.' I was in due course to dig up from the garden many broken old clay pipes, sometimes part of a stem, sometimes a bowl, and when I sent them to an expert he confirmed they were Elizabethan. The evening visits were more lively. Alan's purpose in life being to have fun, he was as much at ease in a public bar as in the Savoy Grill or in our cottage. On one of these visits I suddenly heard amid our laughter and talk, the bleep of a Mayday signal coming from the river. The sender was one of the crew left aboard the *Water Gypsy*. The tide had ebbed, leaving the *Water Gypsy* high and dry on her side.

We went to St Albans to stay with Jeannie's mother and father after the roof was blasted, and Monty, an unwilling evacuee, went too. He was an uncomfortable companion because he took an instant dislike to Judy, the black Scottie, who was after all his animal host. Nor did Judy like Monty. She loathed Monty in fact, and she decided from the beginning to give him no peace. And so there was only one thing to do . they had to be kept apart. Thus Monty was shut in a room all day. He was kept a prisoner and his character began to change. Instead of the winning ways that won me away from being a cat hater, he became like a zombie. He was indifferent to my efforts to play with him. He lost his looks. I began to think to myself how right I had been to dislike cats, to consider them soul-less creatures, selfish and unco-operative; and I began to wish we had a dog. But when we returned to Mortlake, roof now intact, the charmless Monty disappeared. The change in him was extraordinary to behold. He was his old bewitching self. He was boss of the home again. And among the guns again.

The alert went at 11.40 p.m. on June 16th. Rain was falling in buckets and the guns began to bark, unsure of themselves, just like dogs themselves bark when there is a stranger about. I heard no bombs fall, and I assured Jeannie there was nothing to worry about although I already knew the flying bombs, the V1, were expected. At daylight the spasmodic gunfire continued, and it was unnerving because when manned bombers came over there was a glorious crescendo of gunfire; and in a weird way comfort was thus gained. At half past nine in the morning the all clear went, soon to be followed by another alert. The postman called at the usual time. The weather had cleared and he said cheerfully, 'Nice day, isn't it? Lots of mysterious goings on last night.' Thus did those react, who kept the life of Britain ticking.

I was driving along Millbank the same day at quarter past three and saw the people looking upwards. I stopped the car and heard the drone of a V1. I got out and made towards a shelter. Then I saw this particular V1 above Battersea Power Station, and its engine didn't cut out, and it continued northwards, so I went back to my car and went on with my journey. The following day I had lunched at the Savoy and I came out to the Embankment entrance where I had parked the car; and Chamberlain, the hall porter, said to me: 'Wait a moment, Captain, the alert's just gone, and the first five minutes are the worst.' I waited with him, and we heard four V1's buzz over in quick succession, then a few seconds' silence after their engines had cut off, then the crash; and we tried to guess where the people had been killed. For the people south of the Thames, within easier range, the flying bombs were hell. All night they were listening for an engine cutting out, then waiting for the seconds to pass before the explosion; and in the early morning too, and as they washed, and as they ate breakfast, and went on their way to the office, and when they were there, and when they had lunch, and in the afternoon, and as they went home, and as they cooked their supper, and as they waited to go to bed, and as they tried to sleep.

'I was in Harvey Nichols' this morning,' said Jeannie calmly as she was cooking my dinner, Monty looking at her hopefully, 'when the warning buzzers went and we all lay flat among rolls of carpet on the ground floor. We heard a V1 pass overhead, and then we all got up. A moment later we heard another coming, and we all fell on the floor again.'

I would ring up Jeannie from my office when I heard a crash in the Savoy direction and saw a plume of black smoke. 'All right?' 'Yes, it was in Kingsway.' Or she would ring me. And a slang developed among people. 'O.K., it's gone over' . . . 'O.K., I heard it drop' . . . 'This is a near one, get down' . . . 'Poor devils' . . . 'I should think it's Sloane Street.' And there were the clouds, the endless low clouds that summer which let the V1's fly unseen, and the questions which were asked: 'On which side is God?' Thus did people live and think and fear, and have a purpose.

In November *One King* was published. Three weeks beforehand Jeannie and I had gone to stay at a farm called

Treglossick on the Lizard peninsula for our annual leave. In the middle of the first week, my dear friend Jackie Broadbent, political correspondent of the *Daily Mail*, sent me a telegram: 'Manny Shinwell is going round the House praising *One King* to the skies.'

'Damn Jackie,' I said to Jeannie, after I had read the telegram in the sitting room which at night was lit by an oil lamp. 'Damn him, I wanted to be left in peace.'

Such is the perversity of life. My enthusiasm had been drained into the book, and there was none left in me to enjoy the results.

THIRTEEN

My life, after victory came, was not as straightforward as Jeannie's. I suddenly woke up to realise that I had passed the age of irresponsible dreams. And yet the dreams persisted making me puzzled and restless and unsure. It was as if I were meeting myself again after five years wearing the same clothes ... there was the old self, however much I might have appeared to have changed in the meantime. I still wanted to play a lone role. I still knew that my mind would curdle if I were subject to an authority which I despised These were the feelings I had always had; and they were supported by the knowledge that Jeannie felt as I did. We both believed that independence rather than conventional success was the greatest prize to possess.

But such an attitude has to measure up to reality. We were like countless others who, wanting to be free, had not the means which could provide such freedom. We could only muddle our way to the goal we were aiming at, hoping that fate would lead us there. We were not yet ready to do anything drastic. We were content to wait ... Jeannie satisfied in the excitement of her job while I probed to find a compromise between the old self and the new. And I soon discovered how difficult this was going to be.

I pretended to myself, for instance, that a likely method to win our independence would be for me to write a novel. I foresaw that it would be sold for a movie, that I would become a script writer, and that Jeannie and I would then travel the world collecting material for further novels and further movies. The realisation of this delightful prospect depended, I felt, upon a period of total concentration. I had resolutely to refrain from becoming involved in any other activity. I would hide myself in Thames Bank Cottage for six months, and then emerge with a manuscript which displayed the knack and opportunism of a contemporary story teller. That was my superficial plan.

I had not, however, taken into account the after effects of my book on the Commonwealth. I was sought after. I was offered lecture tours. I was offered the job of Commonwealth correspondent on a prestige newspaper. There I sat in the top room of the cottage with the windows looking over the river, a blank piece of paper in front of me, turning down all these approaches, pleased with myself for my determination to do so, but aware that I was slowly weakening. After all, the novel was a ridiculous gamble. Would I not be wiser to cash in on the prestige that *One King* had given me?

A week or two later, and a blank piece of paper still in front of me, I was made another offer. The nature of it inevitably appealed to my vanity. Arthur Christiansen, the dapper, legendary editor of the *Daily Express*, rang me up.

'Meet me in the American Bar at the Savoy this evening,' he said.

'Why?'

'I want you to take over the William Hickey column.'

'Impossible.'

Chris hired and fired people with abandon. He had, I suppose, a kindly nature, certainly an engaging one, but loyalty to individuals was never allowed to interfere with his loyalty to the newspaper. This I knew, and I was on guard. And yet I was flattered.

The following day I was contacted by an emissary of Chris. Again I said no. I said no the next day and the next, and now I knew that Beaverbrook had decided he wanted me, and Chris, therefore, was determined to get me. The money was

155

good, and the William Hickey column in those days was a plum job. Tom Driberg, the best columnist ever to work on British newspapers, had made its reputation; and there was no army of people contributing little paragraphs. The man who wrote the column was out on his own.

I still lived, however, in the shadow of MI5. I had surrendered my uniform and I had given up my flat, but there was still an arrangement whereby I was to operate on certain missions should the necessity arise. Of course the William Hickey column might provide me with a good cover, but clearly I was not going to take that into consideration in deciding whether or not I accepted the job. It was really a question of self indulgence. On the one hand I had learnt, during my years with MI5, the basic principle of reporting without prejudice about events and people; on the other hand I was tempted to experience again the thrill of the chase which always swept over me whenever I entered a newspaper office. I was sitting dolefully in the top room of the cottage, wondering what to do, not a word of my novel yet written, when Christiansen rang me again.

'Meet me at 6.30 at the Savoy.' It was an order, charmingly given.

'Yes,' I replied meekly.

I had been five minutes in the bar when he arrived in a hurry, wearing an unbuttoned teddy-bear coat, greeting others he knew before he turned to me. He considered me already his employee. The time for arguing was over.

'I want your column to be waspish,' he declared.

'Yes.' And I remembered the moment I had crept hopefully into the Manchester office of the *Daily Express* on a month's trial.

'I want you to write about people in such a way that their friends will be annoyed, and their enemies pleased.'

'Yes.'

156

'You'll be able to go where you like. Everybody will want to meet you. But remember . . . you must be waspish about them. Waspish!'

'Yes.'

'Harold Keeble will fix the contract. Three months' notice either side but . . .' in a spasm of extra bonhomie he called for another round of drinks, 'I believe you'll be with us for years!'

'Yes,' I murmured.

'I want your first column by 4.30 on Sunday afternoon.'

After he had gone I hastened to Jeannie's office, and found her having a party with half a dozen people so that I had to take her into the secretary's office, and tell her what had happened.

'It's ghastly,' I groaned, 'I've committed myself.'

'You must be the only newspaperman in the country who could feel like that.'

'It doesn't matter what I say. Accepting it is against all my instincts.'

'Never mind . . . meanwhile I can give you a story.'

I laughed.

'Let's go back to the others.'

My time as William Hickey lasted three days. I wrote my first column on a Sunday, my last on a Tuesday. Between-whiles I had not been waspish enough about my old friend Alec Waugh, nor waspish enough about the Governors of the Star and Garter Home, Richmond, which I had visited .. a visit which had deeply moved me. Indeed it was this particular visit that later made me rush to Jeannie to tell her the news.

'I couldn't stand it any more,' I said, 'I even said I would tear up the contract.'

'I'm on your side,' said Jeannie, as if I didn't know, 'but aren't you being impractical by not accepting the money which you can collect?'

157

'Of course I am . . . but it's a matter of principle '

'Expensive.'

'I've never felt happier.'

So there I was again in the top room of Thames Bank Cottage with a blank piece of paper in front of me, and Monty sometimes sitting on my knees, purring gently. At last I could get on with my work without having outside pressure put on me; and one page was filled, then another and another. A soothing life, interrupted only when I accompanied Jeannie to parties at night; and this might have gone on for the six months I had promised myself, but Stanley Horniblow, the editor of the *Daily Mail*, asked to see me. Once again I fell into a trap.

A different kind of trap. A strip cartoon was required for the *Daily Mail* and I was invited to invent a suitable character to dominate it, then to write the story, and the dialogue of each day's series of drawings. I was offered a high salary, told I could work at home, and informed that my artist collaborator would be the urbane Julian Phipps. The pleasant prospect of working with him settled the question, and once again my good intentions were thwarted. The novel was put aside. Only for a short while, I thought. As soon as I mastered the technique of writing the strip I would have plenty of time to do both.

I had not, however, allowed for the personality of Judy. I have no idea why I chose this name but she was the girl who became the centre of my story, and provided the title for the strip. She was a sweet, sexy girl, and Julian Phipps interpreted her on the drawing board as being dark, thoughtful, and with a kind of sophisticated innocence. If this was the impression my story had given him, I have to admit he was partly wrong. The girl was sweet but she was also clinging. She wouldn't leave Jeannie and me.

She came between us. Jeannie and I went on holiday to a

farm in Cornwall, and Judy accompanied us. Every day, instead of relaxing, we would talk about Judy. We would go for long walks on the cliffs around Porthallow, and instead of talking about intelligent subjects, there would be Judy demanding that we should talk about her. How can she get out of such a situation? How can she condense her remarks into a single frame? Would she say that? Would she say this? The first story was about smuggling at a time when H.M. Customs in answer to my query declared in superior fashion: 'No one smuggles in this country.' The second was about the theft of the Gold Cup at Ascot. Julian drew beautifully and the strip looked good. Unfortunately a cleverer rival had suddenly appeared. Rip Kirby had arrived on the scene . . . and poor Judy was out. She had to wait to be seen until the *Evening News* recognised her charms. As for myself, frankly I was thankful to be rid of her.

The *Daily Mail* for a long time afterwards continued to pay my salary. Rip Kirby was a huge success, Judy was dormant, but the monthly cheque continued to arrive. Perhaps this unearned affluence was the cause of my feeling unsettled. I had the money, the time, but instead of concentrating on the novel which once represented so many of my hopes, I only played with it. I wrote articles for American magazines. I wrote a weekly column for the *Continental Daily Mail* and another one for a newspaper in Canada. I frittered my time, my career time, on passing opportunities when it would have been so much wiser of me to have remained true to my original superficial plan. And then an odd thing happened. I really went haywire. I decided to get rich quick . . . and the source of such riches would be a restaurant.

It was no ordinary restaurant. At the time we all had to have food coupons, and the cost of meals was limited to five shillings, and there was little entertaining at home, and there was a general dreariness about the food which was available.

Hence I conceived the brilliant idea, or I thought it was brilliant and this was enough to provide me with unrealistic enthusiasm, to open a restaurant where nobody ate. Instead, the customers entered the restaurant, came to the counter, read the menu, ordered their dishes which they could see were being prepared by a chef in the kitchen in the background, and then took them away in special containers. The site I chose for this strange venture was in Kingston . . . and I was quickly to find that the idea was long before its time.

I look back, in fact, on this period with dismay. I had had the amateur's notion that my personal appearance would not be required, and that my interest in the running of the concern would be a vague kind of overlordship. The chef would look after the kitchens, a manageress would look after the customers. I did not foresee that I would have to be behind the counter, and that Jeannie would have to be there on Saturday afternoons. Very foolish of me I know, but my initial enthusiasm had deceived me into such thoughtlessness. And so there I would be standing at the counter waiting for customers to come in. It was a distressing experience because there were never enough of them, and the weekly takings were always below the weekly expenses, and I had to borrow money to pay the wages, and I was often exasperated by the remarks of the public. 'Will a 2s. 6d. chicken salad be enough for four people?' 'I'll *try* one . . . I'll try anything once.' . . . 'I could make ten of these at home for the price of this.' (A Cornish pasty at 1s. 6d.) . . . 'The trouble is you're so expensive.' . . . 'What's it made of? Beef? Sure it's not horsemeat?' Perversely, as usual, one remembered such remarks, and not the compliments.

And yet there were compensations. The two chefs for instance . . . because I had found I had to have two. They both worked as if the business belonged to them, and when the two little men set off for the station at the end of the day,

160

I felt sad the battle was being lost. They had old-fashioned standards. Adao Almeida was a Portuguese who had been chef to Alice Delysia, the French actress, for many years. He always seemed to have a white patch of flour on his nose. 'When I return to live in my country . . .' he would say. He had only been to Portugal twice and he was never to go again. 'You live better with animals than with human beings . . . it's easier to find out which of them are honest . . .' And when business was bad, 'I cannot understand it, I cannot. All this good food and nobody.' And if a customer was difficult, 'She's wicked . . . wicked.'

The other chef was called Bunny Pessione, and I believe he was a great chef. He was too old for the hurly burly of a normal restaurant or hotel, and anyhow his artistic soul had been too hurt by the poor cuisine standards of postwar Britain. 'In the old days,' he said to me, 'the aristocracy were the aristocracy of culture. We chefs were artists who served them, and our hearts were there as we cooked the food.' His poetic choice of words became blunted when he continued his story. He spoke angrily, and what he said surprised me. 'Have you heard of Vatel, the great French chef for whom I worked at the Carlton? Vatel was preparing a banquet but when the fish failed to arrive in time he was so upset that he stabbed himself to death in a corner of the kitchens!' Bunny liked to dramatise. He was also kind and loyal and hard-working. When at last I had to tell him that I was selling the place, the old man's eyes filled with tears. 'Fancy us closing . . . after so much heart and soul has been put into it.'

And all the while MI5 remained my boss.

I was no longer an executive so I never went to head office or attended conferences or had a chance to look at the files. I cannot therefore write of this postwar period with inside knowledge. I was just an agent who was given tasks to do which for the most part seemed to be of little importance.

161

Despite this minor role I was still able to observe the mood of MI5; and the impression I had was that counter-espionage was in the doldrums. There was little to do. The ham fisted attempts of the Germans to plant agents in Britain had been successfully dealt with. Why should anyone believe it possible that the Russians could do better? At the end of the war there were only two or three people in the Russian section of MI5 . . . but already for a long time Fuchs, Pontecorvo, Maclean, Burgess, Philby and others had been performing their nefarious duties.

I met Philby on what was for me a dramatic occasion. An important member of an anti-Nazi group had escaped to Britain bringing with him a number of very useful documents. I was asked to have him to stay at Mortlake; it was during the latter part of the war, and I soon realised that the motive of his escape was primarily due to his fear of the Russians. The group he represented were convinced of Germany's inevitable defeat, but they were also terrified by the prospect of Russia occupying Germany. He had, therefore, been sent to Britain by the group to make their views known to the British.

The man himself was jittery; and Jeannie and I found the days he stayed with us very poignant. It was bitterly cold at the time and the cottage was like an icebox; and a pipe burst in the roof and water cascaded through the ceiling to the bathroom immediately below, and then froze into icicles. Hardly the time to entertain under any circumstances. But the man was twisted by doubts as to whether he was a traitor to his country or a patriot of a cause, and we listened to him for hour upon hour as he tried to persuade himself that he had acted correctly. Clearly he was disappointed by the reaction of the British he had seen. He had expected them to be as anti-Soviet as himself, but they had shown little sympathy. Their interest lay in the documents he had brought with him. In restrospect I realise only Philby was interested in his views.

Philby had recently been appointed chief of the Soviet section of MI6 known as Section V; and it was this section which had asked me to have the man to stay. At the end of his visit I had to report back to Section V, and it was then for the first time I met Philby. His office was in Ryder Street off St James's, in what is now a block of luxury flats. I entered his room and saw him sitting behind his desk; an untidy looking man behind an untidy desk. I was with him for ten minutes or so and came away with an uncanny impression that he had been sizing me up at the beginning, then decided to treat me as a foe. I am not being wise after the event. That evening I told Jeannie of the impression I had had, then I added: 'The extraordinary thing about this man Philby is that I feel I distrust him totally . . . and I've no reason to do so whatsoever.' Jeannie still remembers my vehemence.

I believe that one of the reasons for the MI5 failure after the war was due to over-sensitiveness. There was a strong undercurrent of prejudice against MI5 in many prominent circles, and it showed itself in a curious way. People would proclaim that they were being persecuted by MI5, and gained prestige by so proclaiming. 'My telephone is being tapped . . .', 'my letters are being opened,' 'I am being followed.' This persecution mania was probably fanned by Soviet agents as part of a nerve war against MI5; and it was a campaign which had a measure of success. My salient impression of MI5 had always been that it judged a person brought to their notice objectively . . . but this campaign influenced MI5 to be too objective. MI5 wanted at all cost to avoid the stigma of being called the British version of the Soviet secret police. MI5 was therefore scared into being too cautious.

Yet I had always found it difficult to get down to facts with

163

my MI5 colleagues. There was so much secrecy within secrecy. My colleagues were charming and amiable, conscientious and erudite, but sometimes when I was talking to one of them a glazed expression would come over his face; and I would try to make up my mind whether he was hiding information from me or whether he felt at a disadvantage because I had shown I knew more than he did. And on occasions I felt like a small boy unwillingly let into a prefects' pow wow . . . for a sudden change of subject would take place just when I was beginning to be interested.

I had dealings with Burgess but I never knew Maclean. Oddly enough, about this time in the late 'forties, there were officials who were grumbling about the Soviet Union's lack of appreciation of the Anglo-American determination to stop any aggression on her part. Open diplomacy had failed. The Soviet Union just would not believe that we were serious. 'If only the Russians had a spy in the Foreign Office,' said one of my friends lightheartedly, 'he could then tell them the truth.'

But I wish I had an explanation about the Philby affair which would quell my own puzzlement. The recruitment of university undergraduates by Soviet Intelligence was a known fact in some quarters. Soon after I joined MI5, one of the most experienced and imaginative among my colleagues said to me: 'The Russians are very patient. They will recruit a young man at a university with communist views, tell him to dissociate himself from the Party, watch him, and keep him on ice for years. Then one day they will come to him and say, "Now we want you to do this . . ." '

If such insight of Soviet methods existed within MI5 it is more difficult than ever to understand how Maclean, Burgess and Philby got through the net. And having done so how did they dispose of the information they acquired? The Portland spy ring needed the Krogers to transmit their secrets. Who was the courier, man or woman, of Philby and Co? He, or she, must still be in orbit.

I resigned from MI5 on the day Fuchs the scientist was arrested. Before I said goodbye I asked my chief whether it was a bad case. 'Shocking,' he replied, 'shocking.' There were certainly a few more shocks ahead.

And what about the novel for which I once had such high hopes? The week after we at last arrived at Minack, the manuscript was once again returned to me by a publisher.

I carried it down to the rocks, tore the pages in half, and dropped them in the sea.

FOURTEEN

When the war ended, Jeannie's job at the Savoy became even more absorbing for her; and more exhausting for that matter. We were out most evenings of the week, and we would come back late at night to Thames Bank Cottage to see Monty waiting for us in the dining-room window, his cross face lit up by the car's headlights, and we would feel sorry that we had left him for so long on his own. Then at week-ends we would sleep and recover, and be thankful we had such a peaceful home beside the river.

Jeannie loved her job. She was, however, a wise person. She had as much fun as anyone could wish for, but the pleasure from it was tempered slowly but surely by the realisation that the same kind of fun was being endlessly repeated; and that one day she would weary of it. Moreover in war time there was a purpose to her work, worthwhile achievements were to be gained by her efforts; but in peace time she was often made use of by those with trivial intentions Some would try to lure her co-operation in a publicity stunt, others would earnestly ask her help, only to forget her once she had given it. She gradually became distrustful of people; and yet, and this was the charm of her, she was always ready to trust again.

I leave her now to tell you how she felt about her job in those years which were leading her to Minack:

I had been at the Savoy ten years when I decided it was time to leave. But as I gazed round my office after making my decision, with its pale pink walls, almost completely covered with signed photographs of celebrities, and its dark green curtains and carpet, I wondered about the next ten years. Could they ever be as challenging and gay and exciting as those that had passed? Would there ever be a sight so memorable as Churchill standing on a small chair which wobbled, in front of one thousand international hoteliers in the Restaurant and making the V sign while ecstatic bravos were shouted in many different languages? Would the entire Royal Family walk up the red carpet from the Embankment entrance to a wedding reception in the River Room? Would dozens of sufferers of infantile paralysis eagerly crowd the passage to Sister Kenny's suite? Would there ever be such a hilarious afternoon as the Mad Hatter's tea party, where the guests were Danny Kaye, Mae West, Olsen and Johnson, the Merry Macs and Harry Green? Would there ever be such a frantic search for the American Ambassador at one in the morning ... and the Manager finding him (Lewis Douglas) at last in Room 205, my office, along with Derek, A. P. Herbert and Billy Butlin, earnestly discussing the Marshall Plan while I sat and listened?

I still have many of the photographs. There is a small one of Field Marshal Montgomery which was his favourite picture of himself, and he signed it on Luneberg Heath. Trumbell Warren, his Canadian A.D.C., came into the office one morning. 'How I curse Derek,' he said laughing, 'the Old Man has made all his Staff read *One King* then he cross-examines us about it every morning at breakfast!' And then Trum produced the photograph. 'I caught him in a good mood and he signed it specially for you. But it was a near thing ...' Apparently a captured German flag was put outside Monty's door for him to use as a door-mat. He was very amused by the idea, and everyone shared his laughter ... except Trum. Monty noticed his silence. 'Well?' he barked, 'and what do you think about it?' There was a moment's silence. 'I think it's in bad taste, sir,' replied Trum. Monty glared at him, then suddenly smiled. 'You're quite right. Have that flag removed at once.' A moment later he showed he had forgiven Trum for his frankness by signing the photograph. I had the photograph of A. P. Herbert alongside that of Monty in my office, suitable I thought because they were close friends, the teetotal Field Marshal and the merry, witty Alan. Alan stayed with him once at his headquarters and though Monty went to bed early, the Staff kept Alan up to four in the morning. Three hours later Alan groped his way to the table for breakfast, sat next to Monty, took one sip of his tea and said: 'Good God, sir! This is corked!'

I still have Karsh's famous photograph of Churchill. Karsh, a gentle little man, came into the office one morning and showed it to me. I naturally enthused about it, then quite unexpectedly he handed it to me. 'Thank you for your enthusiasm,' he said shyly, 'this is the second copy, take it with my compliments ... Churchill, of course, has the other.' I believe I was one of the first to be told how Karsh took it. 'He sat scowling with a huge cigar clenched in his teeth,' said Karsh, 'I begged him to remove it as it was spoiling the wonderful line of his jaw, but he refused and told me to hurry. So I got everything ready, and just as I was about to take the photograph I dashed forward and snatched it from his mouth. He didn't like me doing it, you know!'

There are many others. Two pictures of Danny Kaye. A quizzical, handsome Danny as Group Captain Mitty, and an endearingly scruffy Danny in his incredible golfing clothes. Tragic Carole Landis, the loveliest film star I ever knew James and Pamela Mason at Olleberry Farm when they were married: solemn James with his dry wit; brilliant Pamela with a tongue which spared nobody. Ben Chifley, then Prime

Minister of Australia, sitting with his favourite film star Ingrid Bergman. Grace Moore who signed her photograph a few weeks before she was killed in an air crash. James Stewart, Ty Power – an old friend of Derek's, Bob Hope, Ronald Colman, John Steinbeck, Merle Oberon . . .

Radie Harris, the famous columnist of the *Hollywood Reporter*, Merle Oberon and Gertrude Lawrence were among my best friends during these years. All three were so gay and elegant, fun to be with, and kind. I have a picture of Merle stepping out of a taxi outside the Berkeley with the hotel porter beside her The porter was in a newly designed uniform and I wanted to publicise this in some way; and so when one day Merle was coming to lunch with me, I asked if she would do me a favour by being photographed with him I am afraid anyone who saw the photograph only looked at Merle.

Dear Gertie, so enchanting and vulnerable and contradictory and feminine and impulsively generous, gave us many photographs; and there is one of her in the wonderful part she played in *The Glass Menagerie*, the only major film part she played in Hollywood. 'And if you say you recognise me,' she wrote when she sent it, 'with me made up as the mother, I'll never speak to you again!'

Derek had first introduced me to her when she came over during the war. And when she went back to America she sent us food parcels, and to me she also sent the clothes she no longer wanted; and in those postwar years when rationing was still in force, she continued to send me her clothes. I was almost the same size as Gertie and the clothes seldom required any alteration; and because they were wonderful clothes I still could hand them on to somebody else when I no longer needed them myself. Shelagh of *A Drake At The Door* had one of the suits.

When she was in *September Tide*, the play by Daphne du

Maurier, she used to drop into the office or I would lunch with her every week. I remember the party she gave to the cast one night after the theatre in a room above a restaurant in Curzon Street, and Derek and I were the only two outsiders present. Derek asked her to sing but she refused because, she said, the cast wouldn't want it. It was a curiously unhappy evening because it seemed to us that the cast, except for Bryan Forbes who acted her son in the play, didn't realise what magic was present. She stayed with us at Thames Bank Cottage for our last Boat Race party, and we still have the badge of crossed oars and pale blue ribbon which she wore on her suit. She and her husband Richard Aldrich were our guests at our last New Year's Eve party at the Savoy. She raised her glass of champagne. 'Good luck to you two escapists from the rat race!'

Now that there is a movie about her, with Julie Andrews playing Gertie, I remember two incidents. One was when Derek and I had been at Minack for a year and things were going very badly with us. The postman one day brought Derek two letters from America. One from Gertie, the other from her lawyers. Gertie in the sweetest possible way, the lawyers with the offer of legal confirmation, asked him to write her story. 'I was given six names of English authors to choose from,' wrote Gertie, 'and I have no doubt in choosing you.' The lawyers proposed a trip for research purposes to New York, Hollywood, and of course London. Derek refused the offer. He never showed any doubt in refusing it. 'Jeannie and I,' he wrote back, 'have given up the kind of life such a book would entail. And anyway, Gee, aren't you much too young to have a biography written about you?' She was playing *The King And I*. A year later, she died.

The other incident concerned Julie Andrews. I went one day with David Milford Haven to have lunch with Ben Goetz of MGM at their studios in Elstree. And after lunch Ben

Goetz asked us to go to their studio cinema to watch a test which had just been made of a very young girl called Julie Andrews. I remember she was first interviewed in this test, then sang a song. When it was over Julie, dressed in jodhpurs and a high necked yellow sweater, ran up and down the aisle of the tiny cinema in high excitement; and while she was doing so Ben Goetz turned to us and asked our opinion of her. 'Not bad,' answered David grudgingly. And so that afternoon I saw a star born.

The Savoy directors allowed me much freedom, and there were no special hours for me to keep, but I was always in my office by ten in the morning although I might have been in the background of some function until past midnight. I loved my job and my overriding wish was to do it well. Sometimes I went through agony when a plan failed. During the Savoy strike which seemed to aim at disrupting the hotel arrangements during the Queen's wedding to the Duke of Edinburgh, a newspaper published a leading article denouncing the Savoy management. The article was very unfair. Indeed it was so unfair that the staff who had remained on duty demanded that they should be allowed to write a reply. The editor of the offending newspaper was a close friend of mine, and a frequent visitor to the Savoy, but I felt it was no use asking him to publish the letter. Hence I proposed to John Gordon, then editor of the *Sunday Express* and who now, of course, writes the most forthright column in Fleet Street, that he might possibly publish it in the letter column of the *Sunday Express*. 'I'll do better than that,' he said, 'I'll put it on the front page.' Then he added firmly: 'I'm not doing this for you, mind. But I strongly deprecate unofficial strikes ... especially at times like these.'

I waited anxiously for Sunday morning, and I felt sure that my job was at stake. I had failed in my press relations to keep a newspaper on our side, and if John Gordon failed me well . . .

On Saturday night I was in the Grill having dinner, and I saw not far away from me the Savoy directors also having dinner. I kept my eyes away from them and I longed for the morrow and the fulfilment of my hope that I would be able to rush happily to Claridge's, a copy of the *Sunday Express* in my hand, asking to see the managing director who lived there. Suddenly I saw John Gordon threading his way through the tables, and I saw he had a sheet of paper in his hand. In fact he had two. 'Here you are, Jean,' he said with a kindly smile after a waiter had led him to my table. 'I've brought you the dummy proofs of my leading article and the letter Now you can enjoy your meal and have a good night's sleep.' John Gordon favours no one, but he possesses a wonderful sympathy for truth. And his gesture took me away from one of the most miserable experiences of my life.

The fact is that behind any glamorous job there is always an undercurrent of strain. You have to be on top of the best, incessantly playing a kind of Centre Court tennis. The rewards are worthwhile if you are tough and have no other interests; but if your ambition is to enjoy life, you must have the luck to recognise the moment when it is time to go.

I had that luck.

The Return

FIFTEEN

We had a happy time in London. There was no doubt about that. Holiday London was a wonderful place. Yet we could not separate ourselves from the past. The past came bouncing into the present as we met again the same pressures which had led us to leave all those years ago.

There were the same languid bus queues, the same barging when the bus arrived; the same surge of people streaming across the Strand out of Charing Cross station in the morning, then nine hours later streaming back. There was the same unbearable stuffy heat in the big stores with the sales staff despairingly counting the hours; the same blocks of grey, expressionless faces on tube platforms waiting for trains which were already full. All these were as we remembered them. But now there was also the screeching noise in the sky to add to that on the ground, and the sinister stalking of traffic wardens, and danger at night. 'I was attacked in the Embankment Gardens the other night,' one old member of the Savoy staff told us, 'and I had to go to hospital with a cut eye.' And another, a chambermaid whom Jeannie had known since she first saw her clearing up the glass after an air raid, told how she was getting into a bus after evening duty, and three youths jostled her off it so that she fell into the roadway. 'And they did it for fun,' she said. The pleasure of London used to be that one could wander at will. How had it happened that lawlessness had become conventional? London had gone back to the days of the footpad.

But Jeannie and I were holidaymakers, and Jeannie had never woken up in London before, saying to herself that she could do exactly what she wanted to do. Even now it was not as simple as that. If you have been away a long time there are many people to see. And so we rushed from one appointment to another, from the Strand to Chelsea, from Chelsea to Hampstead, from Hampstead to Bloomsbury, and back again to the Strand.

And when we were not rushing about, people drifted in and out of the river suite, and Louis the floor waiter brought in the drinks, and we would take our guests to the window saying: 'Isn't it a glorious view?' The same words we used when visitors to Minack looked across the bay to the curve of the Lizard.

Old friends came who were following the same pattern of living as when we had last seen them; and new acquaintances whose attitude suggested they couldn't unwind. Thus some of these new acquaintances, prominent in professions dependent on the exploitation of transient ideas, seemed to show an uncomfortable tenseness. The stakes they played were higher than those we had known because they had little security. There was no escape route waiting for them, as it had been waiting for Jeannie and me. The cost of primitive living was now too expensive. Yet successful and full of promise at thirty, they were expendable at forty. There had been no war to halt the growing up of youth, and so creative business had a relay of brains to choose from. 'All my present bright boys,' said an American head of the British branch of his firm, glass of whisky in hand, as he stared down at the river, 'can go within a year. And I can engage replacements who will be *fresher*.'

Downstairs Joe Gilmore, the laconic head barman of the American Bar welcomed us. Jeannie once had a greyhound called Gold Bounty which raced at the White City, and after one spectacular win Joe amusingly invented a cocktail named Gold Bounty. Indeed everyone at the Savoy used to

176

follow Bounty, and Jeannie enjoyed reflected glory when she arrived in the morning at the hotel after one of his victories.

'What happened to Gold Bounty?' Joe now asked; and we told him.

Bounty was not good enough to go to stud so we were asked whether we would like to have him in Cornwall. He arrived at Penzance in the guard's van of the Cornish Riviera Express, and such was his excitement that I could hardly hold on to his lead as we walked out of the station to the Land Rover. We arrived back at Minack . . . and forthwith chaos ensued. He thought Monty was a hare, and within a couple of days we realised we could never train him to think otherwise; and so we found a farmer who kept greyhounds for coursing, and we left Gold Bounty with him. Three months later the farmer arrived at the cottage door. Gold Bounty was dead. He had died of a heart attack.

'I can still remember,' said Joe, 'the roar of the crowd as he came round the last bend: "Bounty! Come on, Bounty!" '

We were standing at the bar and I asked him if he knew the whereabouts of a friend of ours called Dave Golding. One of the pleasures of the Savoy is that you can usually trace friends by asking at the bar or at the enquiry office. Years may have passed since you have seen them. No matter. You will be told this one has married again and is living in Rio de Janeiro, or another died a year ago in Vienna, or another was in the hotel only the other week. Dave Golding, Jeannie and I had first known when he shepherded the famous Goldwyn girls to London after the war for one of the Royal Command performances, and he had been Sam Goldwyn's personal publicity man. Dave Golding, said Joe, was in London again and acting for Charlie Chaplin; and so to trace him further I went to the enquiry office and asked Fred Snow if he knew his home address. He didn't, but within half an hour he somehow produced it; and I rang Dave up. He came round to the Savoy not long after, where we had a gay reunion. Other old friends happened to come into the bar, and Joe said later: 'Just like old times.' Then Dave said he would send a studio car round in the morning to collect Jeannie and me, and we would drive, the three of us, to Pinewood to watch Charlie Chaplin at work.

So around ten o'clock next morning, Jeannie and I sat in the back of the studio car as it cruised along the Strand, across Trafalgar Square and along Pall Mall, up St James's Street, then round the Ritz into Piccadilly, on our way to pick up Dave Golding at his office towards the Hyde Park Corner end. I had only slept four or five hours, and I felt a little unreal. The car had travelled to the point when it was time to turn full circle into the other lane so as to draw up outside Dave Golding's office, when we had an accident. I was sitting in the left corner seat when a huge lorry behind us, carrying waste debris from a tube extension, skidded on the damp road surface while braking. It missed my seat by inches, slicing along my side of the car, making me feel like a Lilliputian. Then I sat fascinated, after I knew I was unhurt, as the lorry swung round and rose upwards on its back wheels. For a second it looked as if it were going to turn over on top of us. Then with a bang it righted itself and came solidly to a stop. It was within a yard or two, huge bonnet facing us, and leering.

When we reached Pinewood later we discovered that Charlie Chaplin had lost his patience. A scene between Marlon Brando and Sidney Chaplin had proved difficult to take; and Charlie Chaplin had issued an edict that everyone was to be banned from the set. Only those directly concerned with the scene were excepted. It seemed, therefore, that our day had been wasted. And so it would have been had not Marlon Brando come to our rescue. 'I'll fix it,' he said to us in his caravan, 'I'll introduce you to him, and say I've known you all my life.' And the introduction was made.

There seemed nothing particular about the scene in question, but Charlie Chaplin clearly paid much importance to it. He led us to a couple of studio chairs, and we sat there watching, alone except for the technicians; but it was Charlie we were watching, not the others. First he showed Sidney his son how to play his part, then he showed Brando how to play his. Each gesture, every tone of voice. It was a small masterpiece of acting, and when the scene was finally shot, a cabin scene on a liner, the two actual participants were only shadows of the performance we had previously watched. Anyhow Charlie Chaplin was satisfied, and Jeannie and I decided to creep away before rehearsals for another scene began.

We walked across the floor of the vast studio and had reached the door when Jeannie turned to have one more look at the little man. He was among a number of people but he saw her, and waved, then hurried towards us.

'Did you like it?' he asked eagerly, and he was so obviously pleased the frustration of the morning could be forgotten, 'didn't you think Brando gave a magnificent performance?'

He was addressing his remarks to Jeannie as if, strangely enough, he was seeking praise from her. And Jeannie with only a slight hesitation replied: 'Yes ... but we also saw a magnificent performance by Mr Chaplin.'

There is a sequel to this story. Some months later Jeannie received a letter at Minack from the Chaplin organisation She was offered a handsome sum and all expenses to handle the publicity surrounding the premiere of *The Countess From Hong Kong*. She was tempted for a moment to accept, thinking that by working with Charlie Chaplin she would be watching greatness. Perhaps she was wrong to refuse. She doesn't think so. Our London visit had reminded her of the rat race pressures which would have been involved.

Sentimental returns are necessary indulgences. I had been already to Cranley Gardens and Joubert Studios and Elm Park Lane before I went with Jeannie to Richmond and Mortlake; and I found I had no envy of my youth. I did not wish to be young again. There were moments, of course, which I would have liked to re-live, but only because I wanted to correct a foolishness. And as I looked at the doors through which I used to pass, I also thought of time wasted. The pleasure and sadness of youth is that the speed of its passing is never thought about; and so you say that you will do this or that in a year, in five years, only to wake up one morning to realise that what you thought was infinitely prolonged has ended. My generation for the most part was in any case doomed; but those of us who were lucky enough to survive, endlessly remember those of our friends who died. This is not sentimental nonsense on my part. My generation imposed upon the world a gallantry of spirit, a belief in a cause, which may now perhaps be unfashionable. But I wonder. As I wandered round, looking at my old homes, remembering eager, young faces, I thought how lost we ourselves once felt; and how it needed a match of purpose to light our awareness, to release us from our inhibitions. So too today. The gallantry is dormant. The belief is waiting for the cause. It will come.

We went to the church at Richmond where we were married, before we went to Cholmondeley House. We had never been back to the church; and I made Jeannie laugh when I reminded her of my ex-housekeeper who refused to leave our side while we walked, I in my uniform, Jeannie in white bridal dress, from the church door along the stone path to the street where the car was waiting. 'Go away, Mrs Clark,' I kept murmuring urgently, 'go away.'

180

Cholmondeley House had a faded air about it. The paved garden across which I had carried Jeannie, and which backed on to Friars Lane, now looked lugubrious; but the front of the house, facing the river, charmed us again with its Regency curve. There was a wicker chair behind one window on the first floor; and on the ground floor, into which the river periodically flooded when we lived there, we could see through muslin curtains the blurred outline of a dining-room table. In front was the tiny garden, edging the tow path, where witty friends used to loll on Sunday afternoons before austere suppers of liver sausage, potatoes fried by Jeannie, and lettuce; and where we stood with our families for our wedding picture. There was an untidy hedge behind the railings which nobody had bothered to trim.

I saw no change on the other side of the river. It had never been pretty to look at; the cabin cruisers moored offshore were as battered looking as those we had known, like second-hand cars waiting to be sold at the side of the road, and the bungalows squatted, a monument to a tasteless pre-war architect. Of course the swans still looked proud but they had lost the trees on the little island beneath which, that first time I had come to Cholmondeley House, I had watched a pair with the cygnets.

And there was the bridge. Surely no bridge is such an anachronism as Richmond Bridge; and as a result so beautiful to look at. It must be a nightmare to planners . . a narrow, graceful arch, built nearly two hundred years ago, queening the river with elegance; and choking traffic Jeannie and I strolled along the towpath towards it, then along the cobbled road below the terrace, until we reached The White Cross. This was the pub where we used to gather with our guests who ordered their drinks in broken English, American accents, Canadian and Australian voices. Dolly Crispin used to reign there, a wonderful person, who made one feel that she rightfully belonged to the age when land lords were expected to be larger than life; and her old mother used to sit in a seat at a window facing the bridge. day after day, sipping gin, stroking a tiny dog on her lap commenting on the passers by. A pleasant pub.

We left Richmond and soon we were staring at the outside of Thames Bank Cottage; and at The Ship next door, our other favourite pub, where Gus and Olivette Foster used to live. The Ship was now smartly painted a light grey but the cottage . .

'What a ghastly colour!' said Jeannie.

Had we been looking at the cottage for the first time, we might not perhaps have thought it so awful; but through the years we had carried in our minds the colour the cottage used to be, a harmless creamy white, fitting the quiet mood of the old houses facing the river between the brewery and Chiswick bridge.

'It's terrible,' said Jeannie again.

The cottage had been painted the red of an over-ripe tomato.

'Anyhow,' I laughed, 'the rest looks the same.'

The elm still stood alongside the cottage up which Monty once climbed, then refused to come down. The same panes were there in the dining-room window through which he used to glare while he waited for us to come home; and where on Boat Race days the crowds used to watch him, making comments about the pale blue ribbon around his fox-coloured neck. As Jeannie and I stood together we could see his shadow.

I gazed detachedly at the porch and its flat roof. On Boat Race days guests climbed from our bedroom window to stand on it; and suddenly I remembered a March morning, an hysterical moment of excitement when Gertie Lawrence, David Milford Haven and Alec Waugh were standing there.

shouting wildly, dense crowds roaring below them on the towpath   and Cambridge winning by a quarter of a length. Boat Race parties! The tide timed their start at such strange hours, and guests would begin to arrive at ten in the morning, and in the oak-beamed room which stretched across the top floor of the cottage Joe Gilmore, being there for no other reason except that he wanted to help us, would dispense drinks from the bottles everybody brought. They were marathon parties. The Grand National, being often run on the same day, helped to revive the party while tickets for the sweepstake were drawn, and the race run. On the day that Cambridge won by a quarter of a length, Russian Hero won the race, and Frank Bowles held the winning ticket; Frank Bowles who became a Peer and Captain of the Queen's Bodyguard after giving up his seat at Nuneaton, so that Frank Cousins could endure his brief stay in Parliament Jovial and witty Frank Bowles who was one of Aneurin Bevan's closest friends; and whom I first met in Hollywood.

We went up the alleyway at the side of the cottage to look at it from the back. I could not see into the garden because of the high wall, the same high wall which Monty used to patrol; and where he used to crouch, glaring down on the Rhode Island Reds we kept at the top end of the garden alongside the pill box air raid shelter. We did not use the shelter often. We used it sometimes during the flying bomb period and at the beginning of the rocket period . . . the first rocket in London landed a quarter of a mile away. But we were not there that night when a bomb blew off the roof. We were in the cottage celebrating our first wedding anniversary with a number of friends. There was not in those days a fear of death on the roads, the fear came from the skies; and yet people irrationally used to risk their lives for comradeship That night the party was happily in progress though the guns were noisy, when we heard the whistle of a stick of bombs falling towards us. We stood still like Madame Tussaud figures, holding our glasses; and we listened to Capa, the greatest war photographer of them all, counting each bomb of the stick as it fell, cigarette drooping from his mouth, standing by the half open door: 'One, two, three, four, here it comes . . .' Wham! And the place was a shambles.

Now here we were, years later, the tide low, a warm day for January, no traffic on the river, and I said to Jeannie: 'Shall I knock on the door and ask if we could see inside?'

'Oh, no,' she answered, and I knew I had been silly to ask such a question, 'I've seen enough. Let's go back.'

Sophie, George Brown's wife, lunched with us the day of the party which had brought us to London, and I am glad she did. Jeannie had bought a little black dress with a wide white collar from some boutique, and when she tried it on I said I didn't like it. So when Sophie arrived, Jeannie immediately asked for her aid; she put the dress on again and Sophie was full of praise, and I found myself liking the dress after all. Sophie has that kind, comfortable manner which makes you believe she is right.

The party was to begin at six o'clock and it was being held on the sixteenth floor of New Zealand House in the Haymarket. The object was to celebrate the selection by Hatchards of the top twenty Authors of the Year; and *A Donkey In The Meadow* had won me a place among them. But as the party drew near I had a queer sense of sadness, as if I were remembering all my other selves whose morale at the time would have been boosted, had they been able to foresee such an occasion.

At 5 p.m. A. P. Herbert arrived in our suite. He was one of the special guests and we had agreed that the three of us would go together. This kind, humble, marvellous original, had shared with us many happy moments. The continuous achievement of his life had been to protest with wit but without malice He had this wonderful gift of debunking humbug, and he did this without any wish for personal showmanship. I suppose his philosophy was that everyone should have fun, but it should never be fun at somebody else's expense ... unless the somebody was a kill-joy. He never created, artificially, subjects and matters to attack. Wit, for him, was never a commercial commodity. He waited until injustice aroused him.

The three of us stood at the window of the sitting room looking down on the necklace of car lights passing along the embankment. On the other side of the river the windows of the Shell building popped one by one into darkness as the staff set out for home. On our right, beyond the trains of Hungerford Bridge, was the Lantern Light of the Big Ben Tower ... the lantern is always lit while the House of Commons is sitting. Below us on the river, the tide full, were the tugs and their barges, port lights and starboard lights, and as we watched them Alan Herbert started to sing a song from the musical play he wrote with Vivian Ellis soon after the war, called 'Big Ben'.

> London Town is built on London River
> And London River flows sixty miles to sea.

He finished a verse, and started to sing it again. It was a moving moment listening to him, and funny too. He didn't take his voice very seriously. And when he finished the verse for the second time, I said he ought to persuade someone to put on a festival of Herbert musical plays. *Derby Day, Tantivy Towers, Helen, Big Ben, Bless The Bride, Tough At The Top, The Water Gypsies*. It was a good list.

'Meanwhile,' I said, 'it's time to go.'

We went along the corridor to the lift, and soon we were in the hall waiting for the taxi which the porter was calling for us. Alan went over to the florist's kiosk which stands by the revolving doors. And when he came back, he held out to Jeannie two tiny pink orchids. They looked perfect on her dress.

'Your taxi is here, sir,' said the porter.

A quarter of an hour later I was gazing at the twenty books of the year; and in the middle was *A Donkey In The Meadow* with its picture of Fred as a foal on the jacket. And I suddenly longed for Minack.

'Jeannie,' I said, as the two of us looked at it, 'within forty-eight hours we'll be back.'

SIXTEEN

Spring had come to Minack while we were away.

'It has been very warm,' Geoffrey said when he met us off the train at Penzance, 'and the daffs have come in with a flood. The flower house is full of them.'

There was a pleasant reassurance in his words. I was sleepy and tired and a little dazed, and I was glad to be shocked into reality.

'Mostly Mags from the cliff,' Geoffrey went on, 'they've jumped. And I picked eight baskets of Golden Harvest from the wood yesterday.'

He continued to talk about the daffodils as we drove beside the sea towards Newlyn, then up steep Paul Hill, then along the winding road towards Minack.

'What about the donkeys and Lama and Boris?'

'Good as gold.'

'Didn't they miss us?' Jeannie asked hopefully.

'Didn't notice you'd gone,' he answered, smiling.

I laughed.

'You wait and see, Jeannie.'

The lane to the cottage now had primroses in the hedges, scattered drops of yellow, and when we turned the corner to approach Monty's Leap we saw the wild daffodils were in bloom in the banks on either side. It was a clear soft morning and the Trinity House vessel *Stella* was a mile or so off shore, and a fleet of Stevenson trawlers was sailing west to distant fishing grounds. It was a perfect morning to return to Minack.

Jeannie ran ahead of me up the path when we arrived. She wanted to be the first to see Lama because she had the doting cat lover's apprehension that Lama might be off-hand, even give us a can-do-without-you reception. An unnecessary fear as it happened. As soon as she opened the door, she knew it was unnecessary. For Lama was waiting, and when she saw Jeannie she showed her delight by performing the gesture which she reserved for moments of great pleasure. She folded up and turned upside down, paws in the air and yellow eyes watching; and by the time I entered the cottage such was her emotion that she seemed to be trembling with purrs.

A moment later I saw the donkeys. They were standing, head beside head, staring alertly down at the cottage from the corner of the field above the little garden ... their favourite position whenever they wanted to impose their will upon us. I picked up a couple of apples from the bowl on the table and went outside; and when she saw me Penny pushed her white nose into Fred's brown woolly neck, a habit of hers when she was excited. Then, as I came up to them, they began a gentle hee-haw, a whinnying murmur which got nowhere. 'Fred,' I said, giving him his apple, 'I saw a lot of people in London who thought your picture as a young donkey quite beautiful ' He looked at me sorrowfully for a moment. He was now bigger than his mother.

As I spoke the gulls arrived on the roof, and Knocker and Squeaker turned their beaks to the skies, and called for attention. They had not long to wait for Jeannie appeared and threw bread up on the roof. Then she collected two more apples, and while I set off for Boris's hut in the woods she stayed talking to the donkeys. I came to the hut and turned the rusty key. 'You all right, old Boris?' I said as I opened the door.

He was not in his usual place on the perch. He was on the floor crouched in a corner. He looked at me brightly enough and gave me his good morning hiss, then he got to his feet and waddled slowly towards me. There was nothing really I could fault about him except that he wasn't in his usual place on the perch. Nothing really. And yet I felt apprehensive. I described my feelings to Jeannie when I got back to the cottage.

'I expect you're only imagining it because you're tired.'

'Perhaps.'

And at that very moment I looked out of the window and saw him plodding up the path . . . plod, plod, plod on the grey chippings until he rounded the corner of the cottage and arrived at the door.

'Hello, Boris dear,' said Jeannie greeting him, 'what's all this I hear about you?' He seemed happy enough as he pushed his beak into the biscuit Jeannie had crumbled for him.

We changed and had a quick breakfast, and then went down to the flower house. Rows of galvanised pails stood on the benches, each pail jammed with daffodils in bud. In the old days we would have had to force them into full bloom before they were ready to send away but now the public is wiser. There is value for money when buds are bought.

'Heavens, Geoffrey,' I said, 'there are a lot here.'

'Sixty dozen I reckon.' He was already bunching. 'Not much time to waste,' he added firmly, 'if we're to catch the flower train.'

We bunched them in time and by two o clock they were all on their way to Covent Garden. Emily had come in to help us, and as we bunched Jeannie and I told her of some of the things we had done in London. London to Emily was as distant as the moon, and more dangerous . . she had never been further away from St Buryan than Plymouth. 'And did he ever get lost?' she asked Jeannie, looking at me.

I did get lost in a way. Incidents tend to enlarge themselves in retrospect; and sometimes they become more important, sometimes funnier. The air conditioning failed on the floor where the party was held. I did not realise this at the time. I stood there making casual conversation, drinking vermouth, becoming hotter and hotter, mopping my brow with a handkerchief, feeling a fool, and explaining to myself that I was paying the price of being a countryman. I had seen it happen before. The open air type asphyxiated by city standards of temperature. I soon felt as if I were in the hottest room of a Turkish bath without prospect of escape. My conversation floundered. I was off balance. I was like someone who, on being interviewed for a job, had to sit in a low armchair while the interviewer towered at a desk above him. I was lost.

Then over a loud speaker system came a jaunty male voice: 'Sorry ladies and gentlemen, the air conditioning has been out of order. It has now been repaired.' Too late for me.

We went to bed early after that first day of bunching; and I awoke in the morning to the sound of unsolicited purrs from Lama at the bottom of the bed, purrs that had no reason except to express the sheer joy of living. I put out a hand and touched her, then lay thinking with pleasant anticipation of the day ahead. No train to catch. No hurried lunch in a smoky atmosphere. No appointments. No aimless rush from one point to another. All day Jeannie and I would be bunching the daffodils. Geoffrey would arrive from time to time with full baskets, and Emily would gossip, and sometimes our attention would be diverted. The sight of the *Scillonian* sailing by or a gaily painted French fishing boat bound for Newlyn, perhaps a fox hunting mice in the field opposite, or a hawk hovering which Jeannie would frighten away by clapping her hands. All manner of small diversions.

190

'What are you thinking about?' asked Jeannie beside me.

'I thought you were still asleep.'

'Just dozing.'

'I was thinking what a wonderful day lay ahead of us.'

'Were you? I've been lying here dozily thinking we were mad.'

'That sounds a bit harsh.'

'Just remember why we talked ourselves into going to London. We wanted to find out what values prevailed, whether we were right in still opting out, whether our phase, as you called it, at Minack was over.'

'Don't forget you also wanted to have a very frivolous time.'

'I loved all that part of it.'

'But you're saying we were mad ever to doubt our life here at Minack?'

'Yes.'

'We didn't really doubt it you know ... we were just suffering from that mid-twentieth century malady of feeling guilty when you're happy.'

'There was something deeper as well. You had reached a moment in your life when you needed to go back in time in order to reassure yourself.'

'One only remembers part of the past. Truth is always changing, especially when it is related to the past.'

'But it has been useful, hasn't it?'

'Well,' I said, 'I've refreshed myself with memories of the mistakes I've made, and find I go on making them.'

'Such as?'

'The list is too long.'

She laughed.

'But, darling Jeannie,' I went on, and as I spoke I was trying to edge round Lama and get out of bed without disturbing her, 'I've also learnt something else. The art of living lies in balancing, early on in life, one's ability with one's hopes, then keeping the hopes under control.'

'You're beginning to be too bright for me . . . it isn't seven yet.'

Lama was still purring, and I was now out of bed. 'Stay there,' I said to Jeannie, 'I'll make the tea.'

She smiled.

'Did you hear that, Lama?'